Joyce Appleby on *Thomas Jefferson*
Louis Auchincloss on *Theodore Roosevelt*
Jean H. Baker on *James Buchanan*
H. W. Brands on *Woodrow Wilson*
Alan Brinkley on *John F. Kennedy*
Douglas Brinkley on *Gerald R. Ford*
Josiah Bunting III on *Ulysses S. Grant*
James MacGregor Burns and Susan Dunn on *George Washington*
Charles W. Calhoun on *Benjamin Harrison*
Gail Collins on *William Henry Harrison*
Robert Dallek on *Harry S. Truman*
John W. Dean on *Warren G. Harding*
John Patrick Diggins on *John Adams*
Elizabeth Drew on *Richard M. Nixon*
John S. D. Eisenhower on *Zachary Taylor*
Paul Finkelman on *Millard Fillmore*
Annette Gordon-Reed on *Andrew Johnson*
Henry F. Graff on *Grover Cleveland*
David Greenberg on *Calvin Coolidge*
Gary Hart on *James Monroe*
Michael F. Holt on *Franklin Pierce*
Roy Jenkins on *Franklin Delano Roosevelt*
Zachary Karabell on *Chester Alan Arthur*
William E. Leuchtenburg on *Herbert Hoover*
James Mann on *George W. Bush*
Gary May on *John Tyler*
George S. McGovern on *Abraham Lincoln*
Timothy Naftali on *George H. W. Bush*
Charles Peters on *Lyndon B. Johnson*
Kevin Phillips on *William McKinley*
Robert V. Remini on *John Quincy Adams*
Jeffrey Rosen on *William Howard Taft*
Ira Rutkow on *James A. Garfield*
John Seigenthaler on *James K. Polk*
Michael Tomasky on *Bill Clinton*
Hans L. Trefousse on *Rutherford B. Hayes*
Jacob Weisberg on *Ronald Reagan*
Tom Wicker on *Dwight D. Eisenhower*
Ted Widmer on *Martin Van Buren*
Sean Wilentz on *Andrew Jackson*
Garry Wills on *James Madison*
Julian E. Zelizer on *Jimmy Carter*

The Bush Tragedy

In an Uncertain World: Tough Choices from Wall Street to Washington
(with Robert E. Rubin)

George W. Bushisms
(six volumes)

In Defense of Government: The Fall and Rise of Public Trust

Ronald Reagan

Jacob Weisberg

Ronald Reagan

THE AMERICAN PRESIDENTS

ARTHUR M. SCHLESINGER, JR., AND SEAN WILENTZ

GENERAL EDITORS

Times Books

HENRY HOLT AND COMPANY, NEW YORK

Times Books
Henry Holt and Company, LLC
Publishers since 1866
175 Fifth Avenue
New York, New York 10010
www.henryholt.com

Henry Holt® is a registered trademark of
Henry Holt and Company, LLC.

Frontispiece: © Bettmann/CORBIS

Library of Congress Cataloging-in-Publication Data
Weisberg, Jacob.
    Ronald Reagan / Jacob Weisberg. — First edition.
        pages cm. — (The American presidents series)
    Includes bibliographical references and index.
    ISBN 978-0-8050-9727-6 (hardcover) — ISBN 978-0-8050-9728-3
(electronic book) 1. Reagan, Ronald. 2. Presidents—United States—
Biography. 3. United States—Politics and government—1981–1989.
I. Title.
    E877.W45 2016
    973.927092—dc23
    [B]   2015024692

Henry Holt books are available for special promotions and premiums.
For details contact: Director, Special Markets.

First Edition 2016

Printed in the United States of America
3 5 7 9 10 8 6 4 2

For my mother, Lois Weisberg

Contents

Editor's Note

THE AMERICAN PRESIDENCY

The president is the central player in the American political order. That would seem to contradict the intentions of the Founding Fathers. Remembering the horrid example of the British monarchy, they invented a separation of powers in order, as Justice Brandeis later put it, "to preclude the exercise of arbitrary power." Accordingly, they divided the government into three allegedly equal and coordinate branches—the executive, the legislative, and the judiciary.

But a system based on the tripartite separation of powers has an inherent tendency toward inertia and stalemate. One of the three branches must take the initiative if the system is to move. The executive branch alone is structurally capable of taking that initiative. The Founders must have sensed this when they accepted Alexander Hamilton's proposition in the Seventieth Federalist that "energy in the executive is a leading character in the definition of good government." They thus envisaged a strong president— but within an equally strong system of constitutional accountability. (The term *imperial presidency* arose in the 1970s to describe the situation when the balance between power and accountability is upset in favor of the executive.)

The American system of self-government thus comes to focus in the presidency—"the vital place of action in the system," as

Woodrow Wilson put it. Henry Adams, himself the great-grandson and grandson of presidents as well as the most brilliant of American historians, said that the American president "resembles the commander of a ship at sea. He must have a helm to grasp, a course to steer, a port to seek." The men in the White House (thus far only men, alas) in steering their chosen courses have shaped our destiny as a nation.

Biography offers an easy education in American history, rendering the past more human, more vivid, more intimate, more accessible, more connected to ourselves. Biography reminds us that presidents are not supermen. They are human beings too, worrying about decisions, attending to wives and children, juggling balls in the air, and putting on their pants one leg at a time. Indeed, as Emerson contended, "There is properly no history; only biography."

Presidents serve us as inspirations, and they also serve us as warnings. They provide bad examples as well as good. The nation, the Supreme Court has said, has "no right to expect that it will always have wise and humane rulers, sincerely attached to the principles of the Constitution. Wicked men, ambitious of power, with hatred of liberty and contempt of law, may fill the place once occupied by Washington and Lincoln."

The men in the White House express the ideals and the values, the frailties and the flaws, of the voters who send them there. It is altogether natural that we should want to know more about the virtues and the vices of the fellows we have elected to govern us. As we know more about them, we will know more about ourselves. The French political philosopher Joseph de Maistre said, "Every nation has the government it deserves."

At the start of the twenty-first century, forty-two men have made it to the Oval Office. (George W. Bush is counted our forty-third president, because Grover Cleveland, who served nonconsecutive terms, is counted twice.) Of the parade of presidents, a dozen or so lead the polls periodically conducted by historians and political scientists. What makes a great president?

Great presidents possess, or are possessed by, a vision of an ideal America. Their passion, as they grasp the helm, is to set the ship of state on the right course toward the port they seek. Great presidents also have a deep psychic connection with the needs, anxieties, dreams of people. "I do not believe," said Wilson, "that any man can lead who does not act . . . under the impulse of a profound sympathy with those whom he leads—a sympathy which is insight—an insight which is of the heart rather than of the intellect."

"All of our great presidents," said Franklin D. Roosevelt, "were leaders of thought at a time when certain ideas in the life of the nation had to be clarified." So Washington incarnated the idea of federal union, Jefferson and Jackson the idea of democracy, Lincoln union and freedom, Cleveland rugged honesty. Theodore Roosevelt and Wilson, said FDR, were both "moral leaders, each in his own way and his own time, who used the presidency as a pulpit."

To succeed, presidents not only must have a port to seek but they must convince Congress and the electorate that it is a port worth seeking. Politics in a democracy is ultimately an educational process, an adventure in persuasion and consent. Every president stands in Theodore Roosevelt's bully pulpit.

The greatest presidents in the scholars' rankings, Washington, Lincoln, and Franklin Roosevelt, were leaders who confronted and overcame the republic's greatest crises. Crisis widens presidential opportunities for bold and imaginative action. But it does not guarantee presidential greatness. The crisis of secession did not spur Buchanan or the crisis of depression spur Hoover to creative leadership. Their inadequacies in the face of crisis allowed Lincoln and the second Roosevelt to show the difference individuals make to history. Still, even in the absence of first-order crisis, forceful and persuasive presidents—Jefferson, Jackson, James K. Polk, Theodore Roosevelt, Harry Truman, John F. Kennedy, Ronald Reagan, George W. Bush—are able to impose their own priorities on the country.

The diverse drama of the presidency offers a fascinating set of tales. Biographies of American presidents constitute a chronicle of wisdom and folly, nobility and pettiness, courage and cunning, forthrightness and deceit, quarrel and consensus. The turmoil perennially swirling around the White House illuminates the heart of the American democracy.

It is the aim of the American Presidents series to present the grand panorama of our chief executives in volumes compact enough for the busy reader, lucid enough for the student, authoritative enough for the scholar. Each volume offers a distillation of character and career. I hope that these lives will give readers some understanding of the pitfalls and potentialities of the presidency and also of the responsibilities of citizenship. Truman's famous sign—"The buck stops here"—tells only half the story. Citizens cannot escape the ultimate responsibility. It is in the voting booth, not on the presidential desk, that the buck finally stops.

—Arthur M. Schlesinger, Jr.

Ronald Reagan

Introduction

Surrounded by a Wall of Light

Most of *Newsweek*'s Washington Bureau was on vacation in late July 1987. That meant an opportunity for the summer intern to cover the president on an out-of-town trip. I remember Tom DeFrank, the magazine's longtime White House correspondent, giving me my brief. I'd have a turn at pool duty, which meant flying in the rear section of Air Force One and typing up a report for the larger share of the press, following in a second plane. The assignment was "body watch" coverage: I was being sent along, at considerable expense, on the unlikely chance of something bad happening. In the event of an assassination attempt or accident, Tom told me, I should ignore the urge to run for the phone, and instead stay close and record every detail.

The visit to Wisconsin was Reagan's last trip before departing for his usual twenty-five-day vacation at Rancho del Cielo, his retreat near Santa Barbara. I remember bits of the day distinctly: the dawn arrival at Andrews Air Force Base, the preloading of the plane before the president got aboard, and the executive splendor of Air Force One. In the galley, there were pens and writing tablets and decks of playing cards emblazoned with the official seal of the president of the United States. In the bathroom were baskets of candy, toiletries, and packs of cigarettes, in presidential slipcovers, free for the taking. No one fastened a seat belt as the plane took off. The reporters got off the rear of the plane first, so we could watch Reagan wave as he came down the front stairs and greeted the local receiving committee, before we hustled into the motorcade and sped down closed highways to his speech.

His first stop was the floor of a factory in Hartford, Wisconsin, that manufactured hoods for kitchen ranges, where he addressed the workers. He made two more speeches after that, one at a Rotary Club luncheon and another at an outdoor rally in the pretty Lake Michigan town of Port Washington. All along the way, there were flags and banners and balloons and people cheering. Reagan made his case against the big spenders in Congress, who were fencing with him over the budget. At each stop, he promoted what he called an Economic Bill of Rights, which was a repackaging of his wish list: a balanced budget amendment, a line-item veto, and a supermajority requirement for tax increases. The more immediate political purpose of the trip was to establish that, amid the drama of the congressional Iran-Contra hearings and the embattled nomination of Robert Bork to the Supreme Court, he was still relevant.

A larger theme was Reagan's renewal of his bond with the American people. These were the kinds of midwestern places he knew from his childhood. "I grew up in a town with people like you, just across the border in Illinois," he reminded his audiences. He quoted Yogi Berra and Will Rogers and told one of the anti-Soviet jokes he collected. He said government spending was like the grass that grows in the cracks on the sidewalk, citing the example of a mass transit system so expensive that it would have been cheaper to buy every rider a new car every five years. (He didn't say where that costly transit system was.) The day ended with a patriotic rally in the town square of Port Washington, which glowed in the afternoon light. "America is number one, and we're going to stay that way!" the president declared. Thirty thousand people were chanting, "Reagan, Reagan, Reagan" and "USA, USA, USA." ("It was a humbling feeling to be greeted with such warmth & affection," Reagan wrote in his diary that evening.) From a corral on the tarmac, reporters shouted questions about Bork and Iran-Contra as the president ascended the stairs of Air Force One, turned, and waved, either choosing not to hear or, more likely, unable to hear above the engine noise. He was back home in time for supper.

I came back with souvenirs and stories. But spending a day around people who loved Ronald Reagan only deepened the difficulty of comprehending his popularity. Like a lot of those covering him, I pegged Reagan as a disengaged dullard with a simplistic view of the world and a superficial understanding of policy. A few months earlier, he had acknowledged bewilderment about his own role in the arms-for-hostages swap. For any of his predecessors, such an admission would have amounted to a confession of lying. Reagan's present-but-absent quality made his confusion plausible, and a little pathetic. He was too vague for a villain, but surely an embarrassment.

Few of my friends in those days would have predicted that Reagan would be remembered as a good president, let alone a great one. Yet it was at that very moment that Reagan was making contributions to the end of the Cold War that would stand as his signal accomplishment. A month earlier he had spoken in Berlin and declared, "Mr. Gorbachev, tear down this wall." His negotiations with the Soviet leader, which had broken down at Reykjavik the previous fall, would change the fundamental dynamics of the world I'd grown up in: the threat of nuclear annihilation, the Communist threat, and a domestic politics built around these threats.

In the subsequent quarter century, Reagan's reputation has grown and grown. He stands today as the second most important president of the twentieth century, following Franklin D. Roosevelt, who was his first political hero. Their counterpoint is strongly apparent. Where Roosevelt tried to solve the country's problems through decisive federal action, Reagan tried to solve them by removing government. Roosevelt gave us the era of the New Deal; Reagan ended it, making conservatism the country's dominant ideology. But as Reagan's reputation has grown, so, too, has his mystery. How did a man who sometimes didn't remember the names of his cabinet officers change the country and the world so much? Was his intellectual disengagement somehow an aspect of his political success? Did he succeed by performing the presidency in a way only a trained actor could? Did he have some kind of magical luck?

Part of the answer to that puzzle lies in the personal qualities Reagan had in common with Roosevelt, whom Oliver Wendell Holmes Jr. famously described as "a second-class mind, but a first-class temperament." Roosevelt, too, was criticized for his superficiality and oversimplification, for relating to complex realities through anecdotes rather than facts. Like Reagan, he often proceeded in an intuitive fashion rather than a logical one. But both men had a native optimism that helped them depict a bright future at a moment of pervasive gloom. At the core of both their characters was a humor that served as a touchstone of common humanity. Like Roosevelt, Reagan managed to preserve a sense of playfulness amid the burdens of office. "I have left orders to be awakened at any time in case of national emergency—even if I'm in a cabinet meeting," he joked. When Reagan visited China, he went to Xi'an and looked out at thousands of life-size Terracotta Warriors made by an emperor in the third century BC. "You're dismissed," he said, offering a crisp salute.

In one way, Reagan isn't hard to understand at all: he knew what he believed, meant what he said, and made clear what he intended to do. He didn't suffer from anxiety or self-doubt. The search for something beneath the surface has tended to produce few results. The biographer who tried the hardest to find it, Edmund Morris, ended his quest in bitter frustration. Granted access during Reagan's second term that has no parallel among presidential historians, Morris spent fourteen years interrogating a sphinx. "Nobody around him understood him," he said in an interview when his Reagan biography, *Dutch*, was published in 1999. "I, every person I interviewed, almost without exception, eventually would say, 'You know, I could never really figure him out.'" Morris's dismal conclusion was that Reagan simply had no inner life.

That's nonsense, of course. Every human being has memories, doubts, desires, an interior monologue. But it's fair to say that Reagan's private side was buried so deeply that few people ever had access to it. His close friends were few, if any. He was emotionally distant to his four children, who developed varying views about the remoteness he displayed while they were growing up. In the book she published in 1989, Nancy Reagan wrote, "There's a wall around him. He lets me come closer than anyone else, but there are times when even I feel that barrier."

Where does that leave those still trying to understand Ronald Reagan? In writing this biography, I've pursued three questions that I don't think have been answered adequately: Why did he move from liberal Democrat to conservative Republican? What role did he really play in ending the Cold War? And finally, the most elusive, why was he so psychologically impenetrable? In developing answers, I've paid special attention to his words. Reagan was a natural and prolific writer. His two autobiographies, hundreds of radio commentaries, and thousands of letters, along with his speeches, voluminous diary entries, and notes, not only tell us what he thought, but also provide more insight into his inner life than most of what has been written about him.

Reagan's first memoir, written in 1964, shows how an ability to hold reality at arm's length functioned as a coping mechanism and an enabler of his success. He cultivated his emotional distance as a survival mechanism, then turned it into a secret weapon. Reagan's sense of privacy—his quality of liking people but not needing them emotionally—was the core of his political appeal. It allowed him to train his warmth on the broad, distant public rather than on his family, friends, and people who worked for him. It fueled his ideology of American identity, built around individualism and independence.

During the 1960s the citizens of Los Angeles got used to a weather phenomenon known as an inversion layer. Dust and pollution would form a blanket of smog that got trapped over the low-lying areas, creating a man-made cloud that hung low, blocking out the blue sky. The man elected governor of California in 1966 was a bit that way, too: murky up close, but bright and sunny at a distance. The farther you got, the warmer he was. Those closest to him felt he didn't really know them; many at a great distance felt he did. In Reagan's psyche, the specific and the general were reversed. Friends were something of an abstraction to him. Abstractions such as "the poor" and "the Soviets" became meaningful only when

he translated them into stories about human beings. Reagan articulated this in a wistful 1978 radio commentary called "Looking
out a Window." He describes being alone in a hotel room in an anonymous city, watching the rush-hour traffic, and thinking about all
the people going home from work. "They are not 'the masses' or,
as the elitists would have it—'the common man.' They are very
uncommon. Individuals each with his or her own hopes & dreams,
plans & problems, and the kind of quiet courage that makes this
whole country run better than just about any place on earth."

How did Reagan's inversion layer form? Starting from an itiner-
ant childhood, forced from place to place by his father's alcoholism, he willed himself to become an autonomous, self-reliant
person. Denying and forgetting unpleasant reality allowed what
Reagan's dedicated chronicler Lou Cannon calls his "optimistic
imagination" to flourish amid the difficult conditions of the Depression. At one level, he was simply adopting his mother's approach
to his father's "weakness," pretending it wasn't there or that it wasn't
really so bad. But Reagan's fogginess was overdetermined in that it
was physical as well as emotional, accentuated by severe myopia,
and later by poor hearing. "I hate them to this day," he wrote in the
mid-1960s about having to wear glasses.

This was only partly vanity. It was also Reagan's preference for
blur. Elsewhere, in a series of newspaper articles he wrote from
Hollywood for the folks back home in Iowa, he talked about making
his first films. He described his feeling of comfort acting "surrounded by a wall of light" that made it impossible to see anyone
else. This created "a feeling of privacy that completely dispelled
any nervousness I might have expected." Many actors love the sense
of connection to their audience; Reagan thrived on the isolation of
performance. His cheerfulness and positive outlook drew people
to him. His aloofness kept them at a distance. Reagan's emotional
inaccessibility drove the women he loved during the first part of
his life to abandon him—his first fiancée, Margaret Cleaver, and his
first wife, Jane Wyman, whose abandonment he found mystifying.
Reagan's Fortress of Solitude was also a way of coping with the
pain of rejection and disappointment, including disappointment

in himself. In his blissful second marriage to Nancy, who didn't push for more than he could deliver, his fog became a way to preserve his ideals in the face of his lapses as a father and of behavior by his children that fell short of his ideals. Reagan chose to see his family life in the harmonious way he wished it to be, not the way it often was.

In the public realm, Reagan's obliviousness was equally functional. Willed blurriness became a technique he used to overlook moral lapses by the country he loved. Applying a soft-focus lens to American history was a way to repel the assault on it by the 1960s and reassert the nation's enduring values. Tuning out discomfiting realities allowed Reagan to articulate his resonant version of American exceptionalism, his belief in the country's divine chosen-ness and moral superiority. Reagan found that vagueness was a good management technique as well. Setting broad direction and leaving the details to others meant that he got credit for what others accomplished, but less than the ordinary measure of blame when his plans ran aground. I don't think Reagan sprayed his mist cynically, but I do think he had considerable control over it, at least until his later years. He could disappear into the fog at difficult moments and reemerge when conditions were more auspicious. There is something especially poignant in Reagan's succumbing to Alzheimer's, drawn ever deeper into a mental twilight that had always been his greatest protection against the pain of life.

1

Fact and Fancy

Ronald Reagan's father was born John Edward Reagan in 1883 and known as Jack. He was Irish Catholic, which as Reagan noted made him "something of an outcast" in their Protestant town. The family had come from County Tipperary to western Illinois in the 1850s, changing their name from O'Regan in the process. Jack was orphaned at the age of six, when both his parents died of tuberculosis, and at sixteen he was selling shoes at the J. W. Broadhead Dry Goods Store in Fulton, Illinois. It was there that he developed his skill for storytelling—"the best raconteur I ever heard," according to his son—and a fatal fondness for whiskey.

Reagan's mother, Nelle Clyde Wilson Reagan, was born on a farm not far away. Her father's family, the Wilsons, were Scottish Protestants who arrived in Illinois by way of Ontario. After Nelle's father ran away to Chicago, she and her six older siblings were raised by her English-born mother, who worked as a domestic servant. Like Jack, Nelle never went to high school. The couple married in 1904. In 1908, Nelle gave birth to their first child, Neil. Their second, Ronald Wilson Reagan, was born above the bakery and general store where his father worked in Tampico, Illinois, on February 6, 1911. His father said he looked like a fat Dutchman, giving him the nickname that stuck. It was a difficult delivery for his mother, who was advised by the doctor not to have more children.

Neil was baptized a Catholic. Ronald was not. The evidence suggests that Nelle underwent a religious conversion in the time between the births of her two sons. She was baptized into the Disciples of Christ Church in 1910, and her sons both followed her by their own choice at early ages. While to contemporary ears "Disciples of Christ" has the sound of a severe evangelical sect, it was in fact a theologically liberal branch of the broader Christian Church that flourished in the Midwest before and after the Civil War. The Disciples placed a high value on reason and education, but retained a strict moral code, and were strongly opposed to alcohol. Carrie Nation was a Disciple. The context for Nelle's conversion was both her binge-drinking Irish-Catholic husband and the temperance meetings taking place around Tampico.

Dutch's first theatrical performances were in temperance plays written by his mother for her church. These might as well have been letters to Jack. As Neil recalled, "There were times when he didn't open the screen door, he just walked through it." Ronald recalled the positive: that his father loved shoes and was a gifted salesman who might have been a great success in a different era. The combination of hard economic times and alcoholism, he said, left his father a frustrated man.

Jack's search for fresh starts kept the family moving around Illinois. When Dutch was three, it took them to Chicago, where his father sold shoes in the Fair Store on State Street until he was arrested for being drunk and disorderly. Next was Galesburg, site of one of the Lincoln-Douglas debates, where Jack was again fired for drinking. From there, the Reagans moved to Monmouth, where Nelle nearly succumbed to the influenza epidemic of 1918. Next they tried Tampico again, before landing in 1920 in Dixon, where they lived in five different homes. Jack's hopes of owning his own store never came to be. Nor did he own a house, until his son bought one for him and Nelle in Hollywood in 1938.

By the age of ten, Dutch had lived in at least ten different homes. The frequent moves at least partially explain why he had few friends growing up. His brother, Neil—nicknamed Moon because he looked like the comic strip character Moon Mullins, with his hair parted down the middle—believed that Dutch didn't need any. Nancy Reagan attributed the lack of close friends to her husband's natural inwardness. In his own description, he simply liked spending time alone, whether walking, swimming, or on horseback.

From ages nine to twenty-one, Reagan lived in Dixon, one hundred miles west of Chicago. This was the home of his heart, the place that would stand in his imagination for small-town America. With a population of around eight thousand in 1920, it was a community built around dairy farming. He and his brother remembered their growing up in starkly different ways. Neil remembered poverty: sharing a bed, eating "bone soup" all week. Dutch's version was "We were poor, but we didn't know we were poor." He joked about his mother's recipe for "oatmeal meat": as much ground beef as you had combined with as much oatmeal as you needed, with gravy on it. He remembered it being delicious.

The gap between the brothers is captured in one of Reagan's favorite jokes: A couple goes to see a psychiatrist about their two sons, one an extreme pessimist, the other an extreme optimist. The psychiatrist takes the pessimistic boy into a roomful of shiny new toys. The boy bursts into tears, sure the toys will break. Then the psychiatrist takes the other boy into a roomful of horse manure. The boy gleefully begins shoveling. "What do you think you're doing?" the psychiatrist asks. "With all this manure," the little boy replies, "there must be a pony in here somewhere!" The story may allude even more specifically to the year there were no Christmas presents in the Reagan house because Jack drank away the money. Neil remembered that. Dutch remembered the year their father managed to surprise his brother with an electric train set the family couldn't afford.

In his early memoir, Reagan depicts his boyhood as "one of those rare Tom Sawyer–Huck Finn idylls" in which he wandered along the Rock River that flows through Dixon and explored the woods of northwestern Illinois. In winter, the Rock River was a skating rink "two hundred yards wide and endlessly long, as clear and smooth as glass." The trick was to skate against the wind and use your coat as a sail to carry you back. Independent exploration substituted for baseball, which it turned out he couldn't play because of his eyesight. Dutch's nearsightedness wasn't discovered until he was around thirteen and tried on his mother's eyeglasses. In his book, he describes the sensation of seeing the world come into focus for the first time.

Another escape was literary fantasy. Dutch became an avid reader of Zane Grey and of Horatio Alger stories. Edgar Rice Burroughs's John Carter books ignited his interest in science fiction. A 1902 novel called *The Printer of Udell's: A Story of the Middle West* influenced Reagan's decision to be baptized as a Disciple and left a strong enough impression that he remembered it in 1981, when the *New York Times Book Review* asked about his early reading. In the book, the hardworking hero rescues a woman from a life of prostitution and eventually gets elected to Congress. "All in all, as I look back, I realize that my reading left an abiding belief in the triumph of good over evil," Reagan wrote. "There were heroes who lived by standards of morality and fair play."

At home, it was getting harder to ignore his father's drinking. Reagan remembered being eleven the first time he found Jack passed out on the front porch of their home, his hair soaked with melting snow. Previously, his mother or older brother had dealt with Jack's bouts of drunkenness. Despite his urge to hide in bed and pretend it wasn't happening, Reagan knew he now had to face the situation. "I got a fistful of his overcoat. Opening the door, I managed to get him inside and drag him to bed," he wrote. Reagan described this moment as the beginning of his accepting adult responsibility. It also epitomized how he learned to cope with unhappiness, not telling his mother or brother about the incident.

At North Dixon High School, Dutch was a dreamy, introspective kid who "used to love to make up plays and act in them myself." In high school, he was president of the drama club. Acting in school plays, he later wrote, helped him deal with his feelings of insecurity. Theatrical narratives were alternatives to the agonizing reality at home. His motto in his high school yearbook was "Life is just one grand sweet song, so start the music." This came from a poem he wrote called "Life," which expressed an outlook that didn't change much over the subsequent years. The poem's first stanza:

> I wonder what it's all about, and why
> We suffer so, when little things go wrong?
> We make our life a struggle,
> When life should be a song.

As the poem suggests, Reagan's sunniness was not only an inborn disposition but also a choice to reject feelings of unhappiness.

His favorite sport was football, where good vision wasn't critical. Despite his small size in high school (5 foot 3 and 108 pounds) he managed to start as a guard. Being squashed at the bottom of a pileup left him with lifelong claustrophobia. It was in swimming, a sport where eyesight matters even less, that Dutch excelled. He had taken a lifesaving course at the YMCA, and when he was sixteen he got a summer job working seven days a week as a lifeguard at Lowell Park, four miles north of Dixon. His pay started at fifteen dollars a week, and he saved nearly every penny for college.

There was local glamour to the job and an element of public performance. "You know why I had such fun at it? Because I was the only one up there on the guard stand. It was like a stage. Everyone had to look at me," he would later tell an interviewer for *Motion Picture* magazine. The Rock River, which flows into the Mississippi, has dangerous currents, and Dutch frequently had to fling off his glasses and plunge in to perform rescues. Sometimes he had to revive people with artificial respiration. At his father's suggestion, he found an old log and made a notch in it every time he saved someone. At the end of six summers, it had seventy-seven notches. He remembered that no one ever thanked him or rewarded him for saving them, with the exception of one blind man. Most were too embarrassed to acknowledge that they'd needed help.

Dutch's high school sweetheart was Margaret Cleaver, known as Mugs, the daughter of the family's minister at the Christian Church. Her father, Benjamin Cleaver, was in ways more a father to him than Jack. Cleaver taught Reagan to drive, talked to him about life, and got him into Eureka College, a tiny Disciples of Christ institution ninety miles downstate from Dixon, where Mugs was headed. Eureka had evolved into a liberal arts college of 220

students, open to women and blacks. But it was a church institution, with chapel attendance required, and no drinking, smoking,
gambling, or dancing. The four hundred dollars Reagan had saved
from lifeguarding wasn't enough for him to enroll, but he got an
athletic scholarship to pay half his tuition and washed dishes to
cover the rest.

The college was barely getting by as well. Reagan described his
first political experience as the role he played in a student strike to
protest curriculum cutbacks during his freshman year. What's
interesting is how Reagan remembered this episode thirty-five
years later, when he was preparing to run for governor of California
and making an issue out of the free-speech protests at Berkeley.
"Ours was no riotous burning in effigy but a serious, well-planned
program, engineered from the ground up by the students but with
the full support and approval of almost every professor on campus,"
he wrote. As Garry Wills points out, Reagan was a tame sort of
campus rebel: not questioning authority so much as invoking
the authority of the community against the flawed leadership of
Eureka's unpopular president.

In Lou Cannon's words, "No memories of scholarship intrude
upon Ronald Reagan's recollections of his college days." Reagan
started as an English major, but dropped it when he had to read
Chaucer. After dabbling in history, he chose economics and soci-
ology for his major. He got poor grades, which he justified as intentional, to prevent his ending up as an athletic coach at some small
school. What got him through was his ability to memorize. His
brother thought he had photographic recall. The night before a test,
Dutch would sit down with the textbook for an hour and then be
able to pass.

Other than football, where he mostly sat on the bench, Reagan's
passion was theater. During his freshman year, the Cleavers took
him to Rockford to see *Journey's End*, an antiwar play set in the
British trenches during World War I. The drama had a deep effect
on the impressionable young man, inspiring him to become an
actor. It also led him to call himself a pacifist for a time. He played
Captain Stanhope in Eureka's production of the play two years

later. One of Reagan's surviving bits of juvenilia is a short story called "Killed in Action," which echoes the play. The protagonist curses at "a world so ordered that once every generation it must be bathed in the blood of youth like this one." Reagan expressed the same sentiments acting opposite Mugs in an Edna St. Vincent Millay piece called "Aria da Capo." Their rendition of the antiwar verse drama won third prize at a theater competition at Northwestern.

In more conventional terms, Dutch was a fervent supporter of Franklin Roosevelt, another alternative father figure. Back home, the Reagan family had hit a rough patch even before the Depression arrived. In 1929 the Fashion Boot Shop, which Jack managed in Dixon, closed its doors, and he became a traveling salesman. Eventually he found a job in a shabby chain store on the outskirts of Springfield, 175 miles downstate. Jack had a mistress there, which raised the possibility of a divorce. Nelle had to go to work as a dressmaker, and Dutch began sending some of his dishwashing money home. During Dutch's last year of college, Jack received a special-delivery letter on Christmas Eve, telling him he was fired. The New Deal brought relief to Jack in the form of a Democratic patronage job working for the Federal Emergency Relief Administration, distributing an early version of food stamps.

Reagan was also proud of his parents' rejection of racism. Jack wouldn't let his boys see *The Birth of a Nation*, the D. W. Griffith epic. "It deals with the Ku Klux Klan against the colored folk," Reagan remembered his father declaring. "And I'm damned if anyone in this family will go see it." Once, when two black football teammates were denied hotel accommodations, Dutch took them to sleep at his house. Another story he liked to tell was about a hotel clerk bragging to his father that the place didn't allow Jews. Jack replied that he was Catholic, and that if someone rejected Jews, Catholics wouldn't be far behind. Jack then went to sleep in his car. The only time Dutch ever threw a punch was in 1943, when a drunk made an anti-Semitic remark to him. The only time he ever stormed off a stage was at a 1966 convention of black Republicans, when he felt a rival candidate was accusing him of racism.

Reagan was engaged to Margaret Cleaver when they graduated from Eureka in 1932. But Mugs, at the top of her class academically, wanted more adventure in her life. As fond as she was of Dutch, she thought he lacked interest in the wider world. She read his sunniness as a lack of ambition. After graduation, she went on a European tour and met another man in France. She returned Reagan's engagement ring and fraternity pin in 1934. His explanation of their breakup was generic: "As our lives traveled into divergent paths, we would find that it was true that before and after age twenty-one, people are often different," he wrote. "At any rate, our love and wholesome relationship did not survive growing up." Many years later, Cleaver pointed to a more specific issue: "He had an inability to distinguish between fact and fancy."

2

Sign Before They
Change Their Minds

After college, Reagan thought he'd give radio a shot. He hitchhiked to Chicago, where he was advised to try his luck back home. His chance came with an audition announcing University of Iowa football games for the radio station WOC in Davenport. The call letters stood for "World of Chiropractic"—the station was an adjunct to a local chiropractic school, whose eccentric owner had a "world famous collection of spines," a stuffed St. Bernard under the piano, and a license acquired in the early days of radio. Reagan's improvisational ability, wedded to a voice with strong presence, impressed Pete MacArthur, the station manager. In early 1933, MacArthur hired him as a staff announcer for a hundred dollars per month. After WOC merged with WHO, a more powerful station in Des Moines, Reagan was earning two hundred dollars a month as a sports announcer in a bigger city. His voice could now be heard throughout the Midwest.

The quality of that voice, warm and soothing, deep without huskiness, made Reagan a natural on the radio. Being from the middle of the country, he wasn't burdened with any distinguishing regional accent. He learned that the way for him to sound spontaneous was to memorize the opening passage of a script. But it was the narrative quality of his thinking as much as his vocal timbre that drove his early success. Reagan was, like his father and brother, a natural yarn spinner who knew how to conjure a scene and characters. He could also do impressions. At WHO, he performed send-ups of President Roosevelt's Fireside Chats for his colleagues.

His most important job at WHO was "re-creating" more than six hundred Chicago Cubs games over four seasons, based on the pitch-by-pitch account telegraphed from Wrigley Field or from wherever the Cubs were on the road. He described his job as "visualizer," making vivid something he couldn't see for an audience that couldn't see it, either. He called what he did "painting a word picture." He'd describe the weather, the expressions on the faces of the players, the reaction of the crowd—invented but not necessarily untrue. Jeanne Tesdell, his steady girlfriend for a year, later told her daughter about the way Reagan would gyrate in the recording booth, transported by his imagination as if he were present at the ballpark. His favorite story was about the time the wire went dead during a game between the Cubs and the St. Louis Cardinals, with Dizzy Dean on the mound. Reagan improvised an endless succession of pitches fouled off by the batter. After twenty minutes, when it seemed he could tap-dance no longer, the telegraph clicked back to life. The batter had fouled out on the first pitch.

Reagan's fortunes were improving ahead of the country's. He was a local celebrity and man-about-town, driving a brown Nash convertible and dating the prettiest women. Some he took swimming, or riding at Fort Des Moines, where he joined the U.S. Cavalry Reserve to have use of the stables. But Reagan was far from extravagant or a playboy. His lighthearted modesty made everyone like him. He was also a good son and brother, sending home a third of his paycheck and helping pay for Neil to finish college, then getting him a job with the station in Davenport.

His dream was the movies. The plan he hatched in 1936 was to get WHO to send him to cover the Cubs at their spring training camp on Catalina Island, near Los Angeles, and to use his spare time to knock on studio doors. Joy Hodges, a former WHO employee who had become a band singer, got Reagan a meeting with her agent, George Ward. Ward got him a screen test at Warner Bros., but couldn't persuade him to wait around for Jack Warner to evaluate it. Reagan packed up and went back to Des Moines. Playing hard-to-get turned out to be an inspired strategy. Ward soon cabled him with an offer from Warner for a contract starting at two hundred dollars a week. SIGN BEFORE THEY CHANGE THEIR MINDS, Reagan wired back.

Warner Bros., where Reagan would remain for fifteen years and make forty-one films, relied on Reagan's voice more than his body. In the first two pictures he made in 1937, *Love Is on the Air* and *Hollywood Hotel*, he was cast as a radio announcer. *Hollywood Hotel*, a Busby Berkeley film, was his big break. The movie was built around the popular radio show of Louella Parsons, a powerful figure in the entertainment industry, whose daily gossip column was published in the Hearst newspapers. On the set, Reagan discovered a private connection with Parsons: she, too, was from Dixon. From then on, she was a champion of his career.

After breaking off a second, brief engagement to an actress named Ila Rhodes, Reagan began dating Jane Wyman, who starred with him in the Brother Rat movies. Parsons became a cheerleader for their relationship. After breaking the news of their engagement, she invited Reagan and Wyman on a national promotional tour called Hollywood Stars of 1940 on Parade. The musical revue, ostensibly a showcase for Hollywood's rising stars, was also a celebration of Parsons's power. "Oh, Louella, won't you mention me / For a movie star in Hollywood, that's what I want to be," the actors sang, to the tune of "Oh, Susanna."

Where Reagan was steady and good-natured, Wyman was insecure and impulsive. Twenty-one when she met Reagan, she was already in the midst of a second divorce, with three more to come. There is no indication that she told her new husband about her unacknowledged first marriage to Eugene Wyman, at the age of sixteen, though it might have taken an effort even for the incurious Reagan not to wonder why she didn't use Mayfield, her parents' last name. Parsons and the Warner publicity department also airbrushed away her brief second marriage, to a middle-aged New Orleans businessman. The young stars were married in 1940 by a

Disciples minister, with Parsons hosting the reception. Their daughter, Maureen, born the following year, called her Aunt Lolly.

Another advantage in Hollywood was the connection Reagan cultivated with Lew Wasserman, who was quickly becoming the most powerful agent in the movie business. As with Louella Parsons and Jack Warner, Reagan swiftly developed a personal friendship with Wasserman that went beyond their transactional relationship. The result was that within a year of his showing up from Iowa, Reagan, a likable actor of no great talent and limited sex appeal, had three of the most influential people in Hollywood backing his rise. As with his subsequent successes, he saw his relationship with this circle of patrons as good fortune that simply befell him, rather than as something he'd engineered. This ingenuousness was part of what endeared him to such powerful benefactors.

With Wasserman's firm, MCA, promoting him, Reagan swiftly became a familiar face in B movies, the weaker film on a double bill. He played comic roles and the kinds of adventure heroes he'd imagined as a child, for an audience of children. These pictures, made by a separate Warner production unit, were turned out like assembly line products in a few weeks. "They didn't want them good, they wanted them Thursday," he liked to say. Reagan, "the Errol Flynn of the Bs," was the ideal assembly-line actor, versatile and reliable. He appeared in ten films in 1938 and seven more in 1939. By 1941 he was getting more fan mail than any star in Hollywood other than Flynn himself.

In the four films in the Brass Bancroft series, Reagan played a dauntless federal agent doing battle with counterfeiters, spies, and saboteurs. Pictures such as *Secret Service of the Air* reflected Warner's pro-interventionist stance, which became the subject of a Senate investigation into "warmongering" and "war propaganda" a few months before Pearl Harbor. One of the subjects of the investigation was the film *International Squadron*, in which Reagan's character, a pilot for the Royal Air Force, sacrifices his life. Another, *Murder in the Air*, released in 1940, was the last of the Brass Bancroft movies. In it, Reagan goes undercover to stop German spies trying to sabotage a test of America's secret weapon, an "inertia projector," which can shoot planes out of the sky at a range of four miles. "It not only makes the United States invincible in war, but in so doing promises to become the greatest force for world peace ever discovered," his character says.

Reagan believed in his ability as an actor. He didn't like having his career denigrated, as it often was after he went into politics. At the same time, he had a realistic understanding of his limitations. He wanted more dramatic roles and parts in Westerns, but recognized that "averageness" was his key asset. "Mr. Norm is my alias," he wrote in an as-told-to article for *Photoplay*, a fan magazine. He channeled everyman, which meant everyone could relate to him.

Playing George Gipp in *Knute Rockne—All American* (1940) was Reagan's first role in an A film. The modest athletic hero, a self-reliant man of action expressing the American ideal of leadership, became an alter ego for Reagan. In the athlete's dying speech, he tells his coach, Knute Rockne, that when the team is in a tough spot one day, he should rally the troops by telling them to "win one for the Gipper." Reagan's favorite catchphrase was a classic Hollywood fairy tale, since no one called the real Gipp the Gipper, and the football hero's deathbed exhortation was likely a fabrication of Rockne's. But to Reagan the myth expressed the deeper truth about uniting around a cause and persevering against the odds. Another line from the film rings even truer about the actor playing the role: "I don't like people to get too close to me," Gipp at one point informs the coach's wife.

The peak period of Reagan's acting career followed: *Santa Fe Trail*, in which he played opposite Errol Flynn, and *Juke Girl*, where he starred with Ann Sheridan. His best role was in *Kings Row*, the adaptation of a lurid best seller about life in a small town at the turn of the century. Though the story was massively reworked for the screen, filming a novel dealing with incest, homosexuality, and euthanasia was a challenge to the Motion Picture Production Code. Reagan played Drake McHugh, a young playboy whose legs are amputated by a sadistic doctor as punishment for a romance with the doctor's daughter. As Reagan's character comes to in a strange bed after his operation, sweating and disoriented, he shouts, "Where's the rest of me?" In his 1965 memoir of the same title, Reagan remembers this as a rare moment of emotional fusion with the character he was playing. *Kings Row* was nominated for an Academy Award and helped turn Reagan into a legitimate star. In 1941, even before the film was released, the strength of his performance enabled Lew Wasserman to negotiate a seven-year, million-dollar contract for him that was the first in the industry.

Reagan's 1942 *Photoplay* article provides a glimpse into how he saw himself as an actor at the height of his career.

> And right from the start, down there in "B" pictures where I began, through four years of "bit" parts (the "Poor Man's Errol Flynn," they called me), I was sure that I was in the right business for me. I knew I'd get to the top, if I kept on working and learning. . . . Thanks to some good advice from a guy named Pat O'Brien, I played those "B's" as if they were "A's." You see, the boss only goes by results. If I do a part carelessly because I doubt its importance, no one is going to write a subtitle explaining that Ronald Reagan didn't feel the part was important, therefore he didn't give it very much.

In the same article, Reagan lists politics alongside sports and dramatics as one of his major interests. Years later, he would describe himself as a "hemophiliac liberal" during those years, and "not sharp" about Communists.

As a reserve second lieutenant in the cavalry from his days in Des Moines, Reagan was subject to the draft well before Pearl Harbor. Jack Warner had gotten him a deferment in early 1941, saying Reagan was needed to finish *Kings Row*. Advice from Wasserman and lobbying by the Warner Bros. chief counsel helped produce two more deferments. But in March 1942 Reagan was finally drafted. Because of his poor eyesight, he was eligible for only "limited service." With some further string pulling, he was soon serving under Jack Warner, who had become a lieutenant colonel in the newly created First Motion Picture Unit of the Army Air Forces. Reagan was stationed at Fort Roach, formerly the Hal Roach studios in Culver City, where he acted in and narrated films used for recruitment, training, and public relations. He never went overseas.

By the time Reagan was discharged in September 1945, his career had lost momentum. Among those who had overtaken him was his wife, whose first serious role was in *The Lost Weekend*, a drama about alcoholism directed by Billy Wilder. Part of Reagan's problem was becoming choosier about his roles. He wanted to be cast in adventure dramas that played out the theme of rugged individualism—or, as he put it on Louella Parsons's radio show, "the principles America lives by; the pioneer spirit, the sportsmanship, the health and courage." Warner, however, didn't see him as another John Wayne. The studio preferred Reagan as a romantic or comedic lead. Over his intermittent objections, it put him in a series of films that ranged from mediocre to awful. "With parts I've had, I could telephone in my lines, and it wouldn't make any difference," he groused in one interview. In another, he complained that if Warner "ever got around to putting me in a western, they'd cast me as a lawyer from the east."

3

The Only Voice
for Real Liberals

The postwar years were defined by labor strife around the country. In Hollywood the battles began before the end of World War II, with violent confrontations outside the gates of the major studios, and continued until 1949. The core conflict was between two unions, the International Alliance of Theatrical and Stage Employees (IATSE) and the Conference of Studio Unions (CSU). IATSE had a history of corruption and mob control, but was feared by the studios because it included projectionists and had the power to shut down movie theaters. The smaller CSU was run by a former boxer named Herbert Sorrell, who was accused of being a Communist.

As his acting career sputtered, Reagan was drawn into this battle as a board member of his own union, the Screen Actors Guild. Like most of his colleagues, Reagan wanted the American Federation of Labor to step in and arbitrate the dispute. When the AFL declined to intervene, SAG declared itself officially neutral, but in practice took the side of IATSE and the studios against the CSU. SAG's decision to cross the CSU picket lines in September 1946, which Reagan advocated, resulted in the worst violence Hollywood had seen. Actors had to be smuggled into the Warner studio via a sewer tunnel or lie on the floor of a bus to avoid flying rocks and bottles. Reagan was filming a beach scene for the romantic drama *Night unto Night* when he was summoned to a pay phone.

An anonymous caller warned him that if he continued urging SAG members to break the strike, goons would disfigure his face with acid. On the advice of the head of studio security, he began carrying a gun.

In December 1946, the SAG membership voted with him by a ten-to-one margin after Reagan made a forceful case against the CSU strike at a meeting at the Hollywood Legion Stadium. Though the aftermath continued into 1947, SAG's breaking the strike meant the demise of the CSU. Reagan's leadership in avoiding an interruption in their work and incomes made him popular with his fellow actors, who chose him over Gene Kelly and George Murphy for the presidency of the union a few months later, and reelected him five more times before he stepped down in 1953. Opposing the strike made him equally unpopular with prominent members of the Screen Writers Guild who were sympathetic to the CSU. Reagan's position led to a decisive break with the Hollywood left, which turned hostile toward him, calling him a scab, a fascist, and a tool of the studios.

At the same time, Reagan saw Communists trying to take over liberal organizations in which he was active, including the American Veterans Committee and the Hollywood Independent Citizens Committee of the Arts, Sciences, and Professions, known as HIC-CASP. The fight inside HICCASP paralleled the union battle, separating liberal actors from the more radical writers. By mid-1946, when Reagan agreed to become a member of the executive council, Communist sympathizers were turning it into a front organization. At his first council meeting, Reagan joined with Franklin Roosevelt's son James Roosevelt, the actress Olivia de Havilland, and others in proposing a statement repudiating communism.

Reagan soon began cooperating with federal authorities in their efforts to identify Hollywood Communists. His brother Neil later boasted about spying on HICCASP for the FBI, but Ronald never gave a full account of his own involvement. As his FBI file later revealed, he and Wyman shared the names of people they suspected to be Communists. When the House Un-American Activities Committee held highly publicized hearings about the motion picture industry in October 1947, Reagan traveled to Washington as a cooperative witness.

He was not, however, a pliant one. Reagan's performance was agile and, in the context of the times, admirable. He defended Hollywood, arguing that the anticommunist majority had prevented Communist propaganda from reaching the screen. Reagan argued for maintaining democratic procedure and against outlawing the Communist Party, citing Jefferson to the effect that "if the American people know all of the facts they will never make a mistake." Though he had given names to the FBI, he declined to offer any to HUAC in public. While he acknowledged that there was a small clique inside SAG consistently "following the tactics that we associate with the Communist Party," he couldn't prove that any member of it was in fact a Communist. Using a technique that would later become familiar, he deflected unwelcome questioning with a rambling story about being tricked into lending his name for a concert at which the black radical Paul Robeson was to sing.

These were the hearings at which the uncooperative witnesses known as the Hollywood Ten were cited for contempt and sent to jail. As the blacklist emerged in subsequent months, Reagan made efforts to ensure fair play for SAG members. When the producers asked for cooperation with their blacklist, Reagan asked how innocent people would be protected under the policy. Unsatisfied by their answers, he reported back to SAG, criticizing the studios for involving themselves in the political views of their employees. He proposed that SAG make an official statement rejecting not only communism but also what he called the Communist tactics of ignoring majority rule. In 1947, Reagan joined the national board of Americans for Democratic Action, which he called "the only voice for real liberals." The following year, he campaigned for Harry Truman with a speech attacking congressional Republicans for cutting social spending and passing a tax cut that favored the rich.

But Reagan's views were in transition in the late 1940s and early 1950s, from New Deal liberal, to liberal anticommunist, to anticommunist conservative. After SAG's other officers voted down his proposed statement as too sympathetic to communism, he moved to a position of deferring to Congress and cooperating with the producers. His hardening view reflected his additional role as a spokesman for the Motion Picture Industry Council, an organization founded to improve Hollywood's reputation. Reagan became chairman of the organization in 1949, and it was under MPIC's auspices that he began making public speeches defending the honor of actors. Most, he contended, were "hard-working, church-going family men and women." He criticized the Hollywood press for dwelling on gossip and scandal. Actors, he told audiences, were outstanding citizens—more educated than average, less often divorced, and disproportionately engaged in charitable activities. Hollywood, he said, was playing a critical role in the "great ideological struggle" between democracy and communism.

Reagan argued for Hollywood's ability to police itself, rather than having restrictions imposed upon it. His own role, meanwhile, was evolving from Hollywood advocate to one of its policemen. Reagan soon dropped any concern about protecting the rights of Communists. He now favored declaring the Communist Party illegal on the grounds that it was a foreign conspiracy. His concern was now protecting the rights of noncommunists wrongly accused. That was his rationale for proposing a "voluntary" loyalty oath for SAG members in 1950. The oath didn't stay voluntary for long. SAG was soon requiring members to sign a statement affirming they had never been Communists or members of a group that sought to overthrow the government.

By 1952, after five years of battling Communists, Reagan was no longer much of a liberal. He was a "Democrat for Eisenhower" and an enthusiast of political hygiene. He wanted an MPIC Patriotic Services Committee to "clear" performers at the request of studios, a move that was blocked by the strong-willed president of the Screen Writers Guild, making the same kinds of arguments Reagan himself had offered in 1947. As his views evolved, Reagan applied his willful myopia to blacklisting. His dodge was that everything was open and voluntary. SAG would not defend performers whose political views had made them unpopular at the box office. If the studios didn't want to hire such people, that was their business.

In this way, Reagan helped enforce the blacklist while maintaining that no such thing existed.

Still, he occupied a middle ground. Even at the height of the Red Scare, Reagan was never a McCarthyite, making political opportunity out of exposing Communists or intentionally blurring the lines that divided liberals and Stalinists. He also took an unusual lesson away from his experience: defeating communism had been fairly easy. "In the 'no holds barred' fight here in Hollywood we licked the Communists without ever using the word or pointing a finger at any individual," he wrote Orvil Dryfoos, the publisher of the *New York Times*, in a 1962 letter complaining about the newspaper's characterization of him as a "right-wing oracle."

The waning of Reagan's screen career and Jane Wyman's growing success both contributed to the breakup of his first marriage. After getting out of the army, he built model ships and went off to Lake Arrowhead by himself while his wife devoted herself for six months to *The Yearling*, a role that would lead to her first Academy Award nomination. With Jane too busy to contemplate another pregnancy, they decided to adopt a son, Michael, in 1945. Jane became pregnant again in early 1947, and in the midst of her pregnancy her husband contracted a serious case of viral pneumonia. While Ron was fighting for his life in one hospital, Jane was recovering from a premature delivery in another. Born three months early, their baby daughter died after only a few hours.

Neither wanted to face the unhappiness. While he was immersing himself in SAG and Hollywood politics, she plunged into another serious role, playing a deaf mute in *Johnny Belinda*, for which she won an Oscar. When Reagan got back from testifying to HUAC in Washington in October 1947, Wyman kicked him out. She described finding it "exasperating to awake in the middle of the night, prepare for work, and have someone at the breakfast table, newspaper in hand, expounding." She wasn't interested in politics and thought her husband didn't take her views seriously.

Reagan agreed to a divorce, but Jane's abandonment wounded him deeply. He spent that winter making a film in an England still beset by wartime shortages. He found it uncomfortable and depressing. "Ronnie is not a sophisticated fellow," Nancy later said, speaking of her husband's divorce. He hadn't done anything to deserve rejection, he felt, and didn't know how to handle it. What Reagan did with his divorce, essentially, was to bury it, alongside other unhappy or embarrassing episodes in his life: his father's alcoholism, his military deferments, and informing for the FBI.

. . .

Nancy Davis was a twenty-eight-year-old actress recently signed by MGM when she met Ronald Reagan in 1949. Though she had some talent, her ambitions were more focused on having a comfortable family life than her own career. Reagan was at that point an involuntary bachelor residing in the Garden of Allah Hotel, where he'd lived before his marriage. He later described that period as one of spending too much money in nightclubs and waking up with starlets whose names he sometimes couldn't remember. The opportunity to have sex with many different beautiful women interested him only mildly, perhaps because of the risk of intimacy.

Ron and Nancy dated nonexclusively for more than a year. "It took him a long time, I think, to feel that he could really trust me," she said. But by late 1950 they were engaged. She took on his interests, such as horseback riding, which she didn't really enjoy, and SAG, where she put herself forward for the board and ultimately served for ten years. She was pregnant when they got married in March 1952. William Holden, in theory Ron's closest friend, and in reality not close at all, was his best man at the small ceremony. Patti was born seven months later, followed by Ronald Jr. in 1958.

Reagan's relationship with Nancy became the only deep one of his adult life. He depended on her unconditional adoration, and the only times he ever professed to be unhappy were when they were apart. People laughed about the worshipful gaze she would fix on him. Her daughter, jealous of the bond, described it as "a mild state of rapture." But even Nancy fell somewhere short of true intimacy with her husband, whom she described as an emotional brick wall.

"You can get just so far to Ronnie, and then something happens," she told his biographer Lou Cannon. Far more skeptical of people and their motives, she came to play a central role as her husband's prod, protector, and chief guardian of his image.

To please him, she also became more interested in politics. Nancy's views echoed those of her conservative Republican stepfather, which were increasingly those of her fiancé as well. Reagan noted "cracks" in his liberalism dating back to the war, when he was bothered by the inefficiency of military bureaucracy. One factor pulling him further away from the Democrats was the social circle Nancy cultivated in Los Angeles. These were wealthy Republicans not involved in the movie business: Walter and Lee Annenberg, Earle and Marion Jorgensen, and Alfred and Betsy Bloomingdale.

Reagan shared their objection to high taxes, which dovetailed with his SAG advocacy. Though he never quite hit the top bracket, Reagan was theoretically subject to an 84 percent tax rate on income above two hundred thousand dollars. In fact, stars such as he were able to create "temporary" corporations so they could pay the 25 percent capital gains rate instead. In 1950, President Truman proposed closing that loophole and others, while leaving in place a 20 percent excise tax on movie admissions. Reagan complained the following year in a speech at the Kiwanis International club that "no industry has been picked for such discriminatory taxes as have the individuals in the industry of motion pictures."

But the more interesting turn in Reagan's thinking at that time was toward a broader public philosophy, which he first articulated in a 1952 commencement address at William Woods College, a Disciples of Christ women's school in Fulton, Missouri, the same town where Churchill immortalized the "Iron Curtain." Entitled "America the Beautiful," it stands as Reagan's first fully recorded speech and the first place he developed his idea of American identity.

I, in my own mind, have thought of America as a place in the divine scheme of things that was set aside as a promised land. It was set here and the price of admission was very simple; the means of selection was very simple as to how this land should be populated. Any place in the world and any person from those places; any person with the courage, with the desire to tear up their roots, to strive for freedom, to attempt and dare to live in a strange and foreign place, to travel half across the world was welcome here. . . . I believe that God in shedding his grace on this country has always in this divine scheme of things kept an eye on our land and guided it as a promised land for those people.

Note the way Reagan turns the Calvinist trope into a Californian one. Instead of the wrathful God requiring inner perfection and judging the behavior of his chosen people, a benevolent deity was now rewarding his favorites by letting them live in the United States. Reagan concludes with the words "this land of ours is the last best hope of man on earth." His paraphrase of Lincoln's 1862 message to Congress was a line he would use repeatedly in his political career. It came to embody Reagan's notion of American exceptionalism: a people defined by their choice to belong to a nation specially favored by God.

Where did he get his idea that the divine had a special relationship with the American people? One possible source is *For God and Country*, a 1943 propaganda film about army chaplains. In it, Reagan plays a Catholic priest and former college football hero whose best friends are a Protestant chaplain and a Jewish chaplain. He dies heroically in the South Pacific trying to save a wounded comrade of Native American ancestry. But it would be a mistake to dismiss Reagan's patriotic idealism as Hollywood cliché. It's more accurate to say that his version of the American story and Hollywood's version of it shared the same sources in lived experience, popular culture, and political rhetoric.

In his speech at William Woods College, Reagan told several stories that underscored his skill in crafting inspiring fables. The first was about a mysterious man who stood up in Independence Hall during the debate over the signing of the Declaration of

Independence. The man urged the delegates to sign because their children "and all the children of all the days to come" would judge them on the basis of what they did that day. "And no one knows to this day, although his words are recorded, who the man was nor could they find anyone who had spoken the words and caused the Declaration to be signed," Reagan said. Another story, which he told many times subsequently, was about an American B-17 that was hit by German fire while flying back from a bombing run. The gunner was wounded and trapped. After the pilot gave the order to bail out, the last man to leave the plane heard the copilot say, "Never mind, son, we'll ride it down together" as he held the wounded boy's hand. "Congressional Medal of Honor posthumously awarded," Reagan concluded.

Is it even necessary to say that neither of these things happened? They're sentimental fictions whose origins in Reagan's consciousness remain obscure. Like many great storytellers, Reagan cared more about the larger point than the literal truth and had minimal interest in the difference. Already in his first recorded speech, he was deducing his facts from his ideas.

4

Living Better Electrically

In the early 1950s, Hollywood was threatened by the new television business emerging in New York. One of the obstacles to producing television on the West Coast was a SAG rule that banned actors from having agents who served as producers, which was seen as a conflict of interest. Reagan's agent, Lew Wasserman, wanted to produce television and had set up a separate company, Revue Productions, to do so. But to hire actors, his firm, MCA, needed a waiver from SAG, whose president, Ronald Reagan, was its own client. In 1952 the SAG board voted to give a secret "blanket waiver" to Revue Productions, granting it an unlimited right to produce television programs. Only six board members, including Reagan, were in on the discussion, and one of the other five was his wife, Nancy.

Reagan rationalized the decision as the right one for the actors SAG represented. His argument was that Hollywood was at risk of losing TV production to New York. The benefit for actors was that as part of the deal they would receive residual fees from television reruns. But he never offered any defense for giving or renewing the exclusive right to MCA, where Wasserman and his colleagues were aggressively looking out for his interests. The proper course of action would have been for Ron and Nancy to recuse themselves from the discussion. Instead, both voted to confer a huge, unfair advantage on MCA. By 1954, when SAG began extending waivers to other producers, Wasserman had a long head start.

Making matters look even worse, Reagan did this favor just after

Warner Bros. dropped him, at a moment when he was seriously short of funds. He was still paying child support to Wyman and private school fees for Maureen and Michael. He had a new daughter and a new house in Pacific Palisades that needed furnishing, on top of a second mortgage and horses to feed at a 320-acre ranch he had recently bought in the Santa Ynez Mountains. At his low point, Reagan was reduced to emceeing a Las Vegas nightclub act in a straw hat and bow tie, a job he despised.

The steady paycheck MCA found for him in 1954 was made possible by the waiver he'd granted to Revue. It was hosting a television program suggested by MCA to General Electric's advertising agency, BBDO, at a starting salary of $125,000 a year. Reagan began working for GE as a liberal anticommunist and finished in 1962 so far to the right that the company felt it had to drop him as a spokesman. This transformative eight-year period in his life remains underexamined, however, in part because it is poorly documented in comparison with the rest of his career. Nonetheless, it stands as the pivotal stretch when his mature political views and skills emerged. Reagan described working for GE as his "postgraduate course in political science," the time when his conservative ideology was formed.

The public aspect to his role was hosting and occasionally acting in half-hour episodes of *General Electric Theater,* which was broadcast Sunday nights on CBS. This anthology program was devoted to adaptations of novels, plays, and short stories, often featuring top stars such as Jimmy Stewart, Jack Benny, and Judy Garland. Over eight seasons, it became the epitome of midcentury middlebrow entertainment. On any given week, *General Electric Theater* might feature a crime thriller, a romantic comedy, or a dramatic fable: *A cheating wife's scheme for killing her husband backfires . . . Sportswriter Mike Thompson is in Rome to cover a prizefight and becomes romantically involved with the attractive daughter of an archaeologist . . . A has-been actor looking to make a comeback falls prey to a bitter director intent on getting revenge on everyone who's ever slighted him . . .*

The program was a rapid success, becoming the third-best-rated show on television in 1956/57, lagging behind only *The Ed Sullivan Show* and *I Love Lucy*, both also on CBS. The content was controlled by GE, which wanted to avoid controversy and make sure it didn't clash with its slogan, "Progress is our most important product." Often, it would sneak in a corporate message, as with the biography of Thomas Edison that coincided with the company's celebration of "Light's Diamond Jubilee." Reagan signed off every episode with "Until next week then, good night for General Electric, where progress in products goes hand in hand with providing progress in the human values that enrich the lives of us all. That's why, at General Electric, progress is our most important product."

The Reagan family was enlisted to represent the slogan "live better electrically" in their new, modernist ranch house, which was kitted out as a showcase for GE products. It had a retractable roof over the atrium, a heated swimming pool with underwater lights, intercoms in every room, and an elaborate lighting system that could produce a variety of colored effects. There was an electric barbecue, a refrigerated wine cellar, three TVs, three refrigerators, two freezers, two ovens, and a dishwasher with a built-in garbage disposal. The company had to install a three-thousand-pound switch box to handle the electric current. A series of three-minute commercials featured the Reagans telling three-year-old Patti about their "electrical servants," such as the vacuum and waffle iron that "make Mommy's work easier." Dad told viewers that "when you live better electrically, you lead a richer, fuller, more satisfying life." The endorsement came naturally to Reagan, who regarded scientists as wizards who could solve any problem, from cancer to pollution.

His broadcast presence was reinforced by his role as a goodwill ambassador for GE, spending up to twelve weeks a year touring the company's plants around the country. After the Second World War, GE's president, Ralph Cordiner, had delegated authority over its manifold business, ranging from household appliances to airplane engines, to 120 separate department heads. Having a visible spokesman who toured these decentralized operations would help sell the company's policies in the provinces and reinforce a common culture. Ultimately, Reagan would spend what he estimated to be two full years on the road, visiting all 139 facilities and addressing most of GE's 250,000 employees. On tour, he might deliver as many as fourteen speeches a day, starting on a factory floor and finishing as the after-dinner speaker for a local chamber of commerce or Rotary Club branch.

For Reagan, it was a dry run for politics. He learned how to interact with a live audience, and not just perform for the camera and microphone. He learned how to test which jokes went over and refine the way he told them. He learned how to preserve his voice and manage his energy during weeks of uninterrupted travel. He learned how to come across not as a distant matinee idol, but as a man of the people. His views were also in transition. Because he had a fear of flying, his contract specified travel by train. These trips were taken in the company of Earl Dunckel, the GE public relations man responsible for the speaking program. Dunckel, who described himself as an archconservative, later recalled long hours debating with Reagan about Truman and the New Deal. The long train rides also gave Reagan the time to read, think, and write. His reading included *Witness*, by Whittaker Chambers, which he is said to have virtually memorized; F. A. Hayek's *The Road to Serfdom*; and *Economics in One Lesson*, a classic of free-market literature by the journalist Henry Hazlitt.

A more distant corporate influence was Lemuel Boulware, the company's chief labor negotiator, whose importance at GE was second only to Cordiner's. Boulware was known for a strategy of collective bargaining, under which the company would listen to union demands, do extensive research, and then come back with what he called a "fair, firm offer." According to union leaders, it meant "telling the workers what they are entitled to and then trying to shove it down their throats." Boulware wanted management to bypass union leadership to speak directly to workers, enlisting them as "mass communicators for GE."

Though he had no documented interaction with Boulware himself, Reagan was spending many weeks a year in conversation with midlevel executives, plant managers, and workers steeped in Boulware's antiregulatory views. According to Dunckel, Reagan "didn't want to be at a loss to discuss it, if they wanted to discuss it." Over time, Reagan's speeches came to match the message from headquarters about the inefficient, irrational, and meddlesome federal government. After a couple of years, Reagan was professing concern about the "business climate," a term Boulware coined, and recounting tales of "government interference and snafus." Now that he could no longer shelter his income through the "temporary corporation" loophole, high marginal tax rates were a constant preoccupation of his.

It was during his years traveling with Dunckel in 1955 and 1956 that Reagan "came to the realization that he was no longer a Democrat, that the gap had widened too far to be bridged." In 1957 he returned to Eureka College as graduation speaker. His speech echoed his Fulton commencement address of five years earlier: Americans were a people on a mission from God. But now his vision was less about chosen-ness than about technological progress and consumerism. Having soaked up Hayek and Hazlitt and Boulware, he was less worried about an "outside enemy" than about freedom being lost from within through "carelessness and apathy."

> It's just that there is something inherent in government which makes it, when it isn't controlled, continue to grow. . . . Remember that every government service, every offer of government financed security, is paid for in the loss of personal freedom. . . . In the days to come whenever a voice is raised telling you to let the government do it, analyze very carefully to see whether the suggested service is worth the personal freedom which you must forgo in return for such service.

America, he contended, was pretty far along on Hayek's road to serfdom. It was evolving toward socialism without ever choosing it, simply by piling one federal program on top of another. But the risk wasn't purely bureaucratic accretion; it was also placing limits on what individuals would be allowed to accomplish. People trying to construct a floor under America's standard of living were actually building a ceiling "above which no one shall be permitted to climb." Reagan's "America the Beautiful" of 1952 had become "Government the Ugly" by 1957.

Here, to pin it down, is Reagan's decisive break with New Deal liberalism, and the first developed expression of his philosophical alternative. Roosevelt, coming from the American upper class, saw the unregulated power of business as the threat to the people, and government as a hero to the rescue. Reagan, coming from the American lower middle class, now saw those roles reversed: taxation and regulation were the villains, corporations and markets his heroes. Years before the Great Society and the Civil Rights Act, Reagan was framing continued expansion of federal authority not just as wasteful, but as the primary threat to individual liberty.

Reagan's 1959 address "Business, Ballots, and Bureaus," delivered to a meeting of GE executives at the Waldorf-Astoria hotel in New York, took this charge a step further, arguing that the perils of communism and government expansion were intertwined. This is the earliest-surviving version of what became known as "The Speech," Reagan's political credo, which ended up as "A Time for Choosing," his famous televised endorsement of Barry Goldwater in 1964. Once, Reagan said, Americans' main contact with the federal government was through the Post Office, but "today there is hardly a phase of our daily living that doesn't feel the stultifying hand of government regulation and interference." He called this shift in power away from individuals and toward bureaucratic institutions "the very essence of totalitarianism." This was just what the Communists had planned. Reagan quoted Karl Marx that the best way to impose socialism is "to tax the middle class out of existence," and Nikita Khrushchev's remark that "your country is becoming so socialistic that in fifteen years the causes of conflict between our two countries will have disappeared." Both quotations are undocumented.

By the time Reagan endorsed Richard Nixon for president in 1960, "I had completed the process of self-conversion," he later wrote. The conservative belief system he worked out during the previous decade wasn't Boulware's or Hayek's or William F. Buckley's, though those were all influences. It was his own, with some notable quirks. One of them, unnoticed at the time, was Reagan's belief that nuclear weapons would eventually be used if they weren't eliminated. This idea probably came to him through his lawyer friend Laurence Beilenson, who argued for preparing to survive nuclear war. But Reagan's optimistic version involved victory without confrontation.

. . .

Reagan finally got around to switching parties in 1962. His paid television address endorsing Nixon in the California governor's race was another version of The Speech, developing the theme that liberals were inadvertently bringing socialism to America. "If someone is setting fire to the house, it doesn't make much difference whether he is a deliberate arsonist or just a fool playing with matches," he said.

Reagan's favorite example of creeping socialism was the Tennessee Valley Authority, the New Deal planning agency that controlled power and water in much of the South. But the TVA was one of GE's biggest customers, buying fifty million dollars' worth of turbines a year. In Reagan's 1965 autobiography, he writes that when he heard that his criticism was causing consternation at headquarters, he phoned Cordiner to discuss it. Cordiner told him that as a GE employee he was free to speak his mind. In return, Reagan offered to substitute some other example of overweening government in his speeches—there were so many to choose from. Cordiner said that would make his life easier.

What Reagan fails to mention is that the TVA was then suing GE as part of a price-fixing conspiracy that implicated Cordiner. During the 1950s, executives from GE, Westinghouse, and other companies met secretly to rig bids for large customers. In late 1960, after a series of highly publicized Senate hearings, the Justice Department handed down indictments, and several GE executives went to prison. The company also paid tens of millions of dollars in fines and civil settlements. Its stock price dropped 40 percent. The real story of GE and the TVA in 1960 wasn't about a corporation

being timid about criticizing the government. It was about a company that got caught trying to cheat the government. But Reagan
had by that time developed a blind spot about corporate abuse,
one that paralleled his inability to see government as a force for
good.

In March 1962, General Electric vice president J. Stanford
Smith informed Reagan's agent that the company was dropping
him and its television program, comparing it to Cadillac making
model changes "to sustain public interest." That *General Electric
Theater* was losing ratings to *Bonanza* in the same time slot on NBC,
combined with the increased cost of the program, provided an
excuse that Reagan didn't accept. He wrote to friends that government officials had pressured GE to fire him, after first trying to get
him to shut up about politics and just sell toasters, which he
wouldn't do. In a series of letters, GE officials insisted that they
hadn't been pressured and attempted conciliation. "In token of our
appreciation for your personal interest, we would like to replace the
appliances you now have in your home with our newest models,"
Smith wrote Reagan.

But neither the TVA nor the ratings were likely the whole reason that GE dumped Reagan. While the aftermath of the price-
fixing scandal was still playing out, Reagan emerged as the linchpin
in another criminal antitrust investigation in early 1962, this one
targeting Hollywood. At issue was what the Screen Actors Guild
had done for MCA. With the help of the "blanket waiver," MCA
had become "the octopus," a quasi-monopoly controlling 60 percent of the entertainment business. Given that Reagan had signed
the waiver as president of SAG in 1952, he was at the center of
what was now a budding scandal. The U.S. attorney general, Robert
Kennedy, convened a federal grand jury in Los Angeles to consider
criminal charges.

Reagan was called to testify on February 5, 1962. He was his
charming self with the jury, apologizing for not wearing a tie
because he'd come straight from a set. On the crucial point of SAG's
decision to grant MCA's blanket waiver, his testimony was one "I
don't recall" after another. Reagan claimed he couldn't remember

the details of the waiver because he'd gone on his honeymoon in 1952. He couldn't remember agreeing to extend it in 1954 because he'd been in Glacier National Park making *Cattle Queen of Montana*. His forgiving fog hid the gap between the wrong thing he had done at a time of financial pressure and the ethical person he believed himself to be.

The grand jury investigation did not yield indictments. However, a civil antitrust case against MCA named SAG (and, by implication, Reagan) as a coconspirator. MCA settled that suit with the Justice Department by agreeing to sell off its talent agency, which, thanks to the new opportunities afforded by the blanket waiver, had become a minor part of its business. In his 1965 book, Reagan expresses outrage at this unwarranted government interference, complaining that the breakup of MCA left actors without representation—though the spun-off talent agency continued to represent him and most others. Whatever the merits of the case, it provides the missing explanation for Reagan's firing. GE surely didn't want a spokesman enmeshed in an antitrust scandal and battling with the U.S. attorney general as it rebuilt after a parallel scandal of its own. Reagan made the connection himself in his grand jury testimony, reminding the U.S. attorney questioning him that GE had fired the employees "you gentlemen were engaged with recently"—that is, those sent to prison for price fixing.

Reagan's myopia now extended to all forms of corporate malfeasance; it's hard to find an example of him criticizing business thereafter. What he saw instead was government meddling in legitimate enterprise. After Robert Kennedy subpoenaed Reagan's tax returns from 1952 to 1955, hoping to find evidence of a payoff from MCA, Reagan told his children that Kennedy had pressured GE to cancel his program because of his politics. He maintained that had the great Ralph Cordiner not retired from GE by that time, he never would have been let go. But Cordiner didn't retire until the end of 1963. He was the man who fired Ronald Reagan.

5

I've Never Played a Governor

Reagan's mother died in 1962, of what was apparently Alzheimer's disease, at the age of seventy-nine. This was the central relationship of his first fifty years and remains the most obscure. Nelle left no account of it, and his tributes to her are without texture. Evidence suggests that until he met Nancy—whom he also called Mommie and Mother—Nelle was the only person Reagan trusted absolutely. This insularity is the natural instinct of the child of an alcoholic. Having won stability and success through his own efforts, Reagan was loath to let his happiness depend on anyone else. Though he had abandoned his father's politics, he saw no cause to reexamine the faith of his mother, which had served him well. He held on to her religious beliefs, attending her church, following her practice of tithing, and maintaining her quaint distaste for taking the Lord's name in vain, writing d— and h— in his letters.

He never had the same kind of closeness with his own children. He kept them, like his friends, at a self-protective distance with his bottomless good cheer and repetitive stories. The two from his first marriage were hurt by his physical absence; the two from his second by his emotional distance. After his divorce from Jane Wyman, Maureen and Michael struggled to insert themselves back into his life. Maureen, born in 1941, was frustrated that Nancy and her father's early political advisers regarded her as an unhelpful reminder of his divorce. She became a political acolyte. After an unsuccessful acting career, she ran for the Senate from California in

1982 and lost in the primary. Between her second and third mar-
riages, she moved into the White House, where she wasn't shy about
telling people what to do. She would die of skin cancer in 2001, at
the age of sixty.

Reagan had much less contact with his adopted son, Michael,
who was born in 1945. As a teenager, he was allowed to stay in the
Pacific Palisades house on weekends, but Nancy made him feel
unwelcome and forced him to sleep on a pullout couch. At his
graduation from an Arizona boarding school, the commencement
speaker introduced himself to him:

> "My name is Ronald Reagan," Dad said. "What's yours?"
> I took off my mortar board. "Remember me?" I said. "I'm
> your son Mike."
> "Oh," said Dad. "I didn't recognize you."

Michael eventually adopted a strategy similar to that of his older
sister, Maureen, becoming a keeper of the Reagan flame on right-
wing talk radio and attacking his younger half siblings when they
suggested that their father might suffer from any imperfection.

Patti, born in 1952, gave her parents the most trouble. Growing
up, she claimed that her father had turned a blind eye to Nancy's
addiction to pills and physical abuse of her. In her twenties, when
Patti mustered the courage to tell her father about her mother hit-
ting her, he refused to believe her. "Why do you make these things
up about your mother?" he said. "I couldn't find my father—he was
there but not there," Patti writes.

Ron Jr., born in 1958, spent the most time with his father,
who was largely done with movies but had not yet embarked on a
political career during his son's formative years. But he, too, was
marked by his father's remoteness. "I could share an hour of warm
camaraderie with Dad, then once I'd walked out the door, get
the uncanny feeling I'd disappeared into the wings of his mind's
stage, like a character no longer necessary to the ongoing story
line," he writes in his 2011 memoir, *My Father at 100*. When Ron
Jr. declared that he didn't believe in God and wanted to drop out

of Yale to become a ballet dancer, his father asked William F. Buckley Jr. to help steer him straight. Nancy was more upset when he married a woman six years his senior.

At home in the GE-outfitted house, the children saw how eager their father was to be involved in politics—and how eager he was not to look eager. He spent much of 1964 writing a memoir, with help from a ghostwriter, to explain his move toward conservative politics. Published in April 1965, *Where's the Rest of Me?* never became a best seller. After Reagan declared his candidacy for governor of California later that year, his political advisers decided that the book was unhelpful, in part because it was too open about his divorce. They gave out copies to reporters and encouraged them to quote from it extensively—ensuring that none would. Still, it remains a compendium of character clues. Reagan's calculated presentation of self at the age of fifty-three is a carapace of good nature, moral lessons, and happy endings. There is no other self to be found behind this constructed one. Facts in the book are unreliable. Yet Reagan never seems to mislead with calculation. His chief deception is the self-deception that, despite his evident inability to form deep relationships, he is never unhappy.

Reagan had gotten to know Senator Barry Goldwater through Arizona vacations with his in-laws—Nancy's stepfather was a socially prominent, politically conservative Chicago surgeon. When Goldwater asked him to help out with his 1964 presidential campaign, Reagan initially demurred, getting his brother Neil's advertising agency involved instead. But after Holmes Tuttle, a wealthy and well-connected Los Angeles automobile dealer, offered to finance a televised speech, Reagan was eager to oblige. Tuttle was another supremely useful friend, playing as great a role at the outset of Reagan's political career as Lew Wasserman did for him in Hollywood. Once the speech was filmed, Reagan pressured Goldwater to let it air, over the objections of campaign aides who thought it would reinforce the presidential candidate's right-wing image.

The twenty-eight-minute paid political message, which was broadcast a week before the election, launched Reagan's political career. Recorded before a live audience, "A Time for Choosing" represented the culmination of the views he had been developing for a decade. The choice he posed was between libertarianism—what he called "the maximum of individual freedom consistent with order"—and "the ant heap of totalitarianism." Reagan's indictment of Washington substituted a grin for Goldwater's grimace. Instead of speaking in abstractions, he lampooned instances of failure and waste, such as a foreign aid program that spent two million dollars on a yacht for the Ethiopian dictator Haile Selassie. "Actually, a government bureau is the nearest thing to eternal life we'll ever see on this earth," he joked. Reagan concluded by borrowing his favorite lines from Franklin Roosevelt and Abraham Lincoln: "You and I have a rendezvous with destiny. We'll preserve for our children this, the last best hope of man on earth, or we'll sentence them to take the last step into a thousand years of darkness."

David Broder, a *Washington Post* columnist, later called this "the most successful political debut since William Jennings Bryan electrified the 1896 Democratic convention with his 'Cross of Gold' speech." It generated a million dollars in contributions to Goldwater and immediately put Reagan's name into circulation for the California governorship. After Goldwater's defeat, Tuttle convened a group of wealthy businessmen in Palm Springs to help Reagan mount a challenge to Edmund G. "Pat" Brown, the Democratic incumbent, who would be seeking a third term in 1966. Reagan liked to describe this circle of patrons, which became known as his Kitchen Cabinet, as having drafted him to run. It was always important to him to make a show of his reluctance, postponing a decision and seeming unsure before agreeing to make "the sacrifice of running for governor." After finally declaring his candidacy, he insisted that he was not a politician but rather a "citizen-politician," stepping in to clean up the mess made by the professionals. Like Cincinnatus, he was not acting out of personal ambition but answering a summons, longing for the day he could return to honest, physical work at his ranch.

Tuttle recruited the California-based political consulting team of Stuart Spencer and Bill Roberts, who rated Reagan a long shot in the Republican primary against George Christopher, the two-term mayor of San Francisco. But Reagan was comfortable with the press from his days in Hollywood, and he knew how to handle an audience. He followed directions well and knew to keep political machinations hidden. He was adept at ducking criticism. When Christopher went on the offensive, Reagan invoked state Republican chairman Gaylord Parkinson's "Eleventh Commandment": Thou shalt not attack a fellow Republican. Deploying this line, he was able to trounce Christopher and train his fire on Brown, who was bogged down in his own primary challenge. Brown made every mistake later opponents would: he patronized Reagan as an airhead actor, ridiculed him for his inexperience in government, and painted him as a dangerous extremist. When he tried to link Reagan to the John Birch Society, Reagan elegantly sidestepped: "Any member of the society who supports me will be buying my philosophy. I won't be buying theirs."

While Brown cast Reagan as far right, Reagan was playing to the center, promising to "squeeze, cut and trim" government without challenging popular benefits such as the state's generous unemployment insurance program. But in 1966, the ground was shifting fast, and much of Reagan's attention went to a new radical threat he identified as a licentious version of the old Communist threat in Hollywood. He called the free-speech movement at Berkeley the "filthy speech movement," conjuring up sex-and-drug orgies "so vile that I cannot describe them to you." In the months leading up to the election, he continued, elaborately, to refuse to describe them. On Election Day, Reagan's margin of victory was 1 million votes out of 6.5 million cast. Asked what he was going to do in office, he quipped, "I don't know. I've never played a governor."

Reagan had run on the motto of a "Creative Society," in which government would support private initiative rather than supplanting it. In practice, his vision quickly gave way to the realities of governing. As if in confirmation of his critique, he was thrown immediately into a mess created by liberal irresponsibility. The Democratic legislature had moved the start of the fiscal year, enabling it to spend fifteen months' worth of revenue in the twelve months ending in June 1967, which left a three-month shortfall for

Reagan as a "Welcome to Sacramento" present. He initially proposed handling the problem with a detail-free, 10 percent across-
the-board spending cut. When that provoked near-universal
opposition, he offered up a huge, one-billion-dollar tax increase.
Reagan was shrewd in tying the increase to a smaller property tax
cut, seizing on a stalled Democratic proposal and making it his
own. He blamed the tax increase on his predecessor while taking
credit for the reduction. Creating a buffer at the outset enabled him
to oppose tax increases for the rest of his term.

The new governor shunned conflict and hated firing people.
Eight months into his first term, his senior staff brought him an
elaborate bill of charges accusing Phil Battaglia, his first chief of
staff, of homosexual activity. Reagan, whose social circle with Nancy
was enlivened by closeted gay men, chose to ignore the issue. His
senior staff disagreed and, in frustration, finally turned to Holmes
Tuttle to fire Battaglia on the governor's behalf. As Reagan told
William Clark, who succeeded Battaglia as chief of staff, "You
never shoot your own horse. Your neighbor does it for you." Reagan's
technique of distancing himself from unpleasantness in governing
was consistent with every other aspect of his life.

Reagan's remove made a strong chief of staff essential. For most
of his first term, Clark filled the role. A laconic lawyer and rancher
who bonded with Reagan over their shared love of horseback riding,
Clark learned to protect Reagan from too much policy detail. He
kept the decision memos he sent Reagan to a single page. Michael
Deaver, the director of administration and keeper of the governor's
schedule, was Clark's opposite. Urbane and gossipy, with a receding
hairline and oversize tortoiseshell glasses, he might be found after
a few drinks playing show tunes on the piano. Deaver soon became
the aide closest to Nancy. The third key figure in Reagan's office was
Edwin Meese III, who became chief of staff in 1969 after Reagan
made Clark a judge. With his jolly, rumpled manner and the smooth,
puffed-up appearance of a pudgy cartoon character, Meese tended
to be dismissed by the press as a mere factotum. Yet he played a
powerful role in shaping Reagan's policies, even if his disorgani-
zation sometimes undermined his efforts.

Reagan's focus remained on the big picture, setting basic direction and letting aides handle the details. He loved the public role of governor, making speeches about the greatness of the state and the excesses of its bureaucracy. His gift for persuasion was exceeded only by his belief in his power to persuade anyone. In his desk files at the Ronald Reagan Presidential Library is a translation of a first-term interview with *Pravda*. "An audience was given to me by the governor of California, Ronald Reagan, a man famous to some extent for his, to say the least, extremely right wing views," the correspondent, Yuri Zhukov, wrote. ". . . Ronald Reagan receives the representative of 'Pravda' extremely graciously—one feels that it gives him pleasure to point out to a Soviet Communist how great and rich his state is."

In 1969, Reagan's national profile was defined by his decision to call out the National Guard to end the occupation of People's Park at Berkeley. As the protests expanded to other campuses and turned more violent, Reagan focused on Communist connections and reformulated his stance on Hollywood radicals: tolerance for peaceful dissent, but none for subversion. "Observe the Rules or Get Out," a line he had used during his campaign, hung as a sign on his door in Sacramento. But in contrast to Nixon and other contemporaries on the right, Reagan managed to be good-natured in his moralizing. He even seemed to enjoy jousting with hippies, people, he said, who "dress like Tarzan, have hair like Jane, and smell like Cheetah." At UC Santa Cruz, a bearded demonstrator stuck his face against the window of the governor's limousine and shouted, "We are the future!" Reagan scribbled a response and held it to the glass: "I'll sell my bonds."

In challenging the student protesters, Reagan appeared to be setting the stage for a presidential campaign in 1968. He made frequent appearances at GOP showcases and fenced with the press about whether he might run. Positioning himself to the right of the front-runner Richard Nixon, he argued for escalating the Vietnam War. But Reagan's 1968 campaign never got off the ground, in part because of his reluctance to appear ambitious, and in part because of the distraction of the "homosexual" scandal after the reason for

Battaglia's firing became known. Reagan's plan was to have his name placed in nomination as a favorite-son candidate and then "run like hell" if Governor Nelson Rockefeller of New York denied Nixon the nomination on the first ballot. The flaw in this plan was that without a conservative primary challenger, Nixon was locking up enough delegates to win the nomination outright. At the Republican convention in Miami, just when Reagan should have accepted the inevitable, he announced a doomed candidacy. His first presidential campaign lasted less than twenty-four hours.

Back in Sacramento, Reagan was building a moderate record at odds with his conservative rhetoric. He had run on repealing a state fair housing act, arguing that people should be free to sell or not sell their homes to whomever they wished. In office, he quietly let the matter drop. The 1967 "therapeutic" abortion bill he signed effectively legalized abortion in California and played a role in doing so nationally. He compromised with the university regents about budget cuts and tuition charges, more than doubling state spending on higher education during his time in office. And despite his anti-environmental rhetoric, he added 145,000 acres to the state park system, protected rivers, and signed the strictest emissions regulations in the country. "Anytime I can get 70 percent of what I'm asking for out of a hostile legislative body, I'll take it," he once told an aide. "I figure that it will work well enough for me to go back later and get a little more of it here and a little more of it there."

This pragmatism set the stage for his reelection in 1970. Reagan refused to debate his opponent, Jesse Unruh, while saturating the airwaves with ads about California's greatness. His priority was reforming welfare, which he cast as bad for taxpayers and bad for recipients. California's rolls had swollen from 375,000 in 1963 to more than four times that in 1970, and were increasing at a rate of 40,000 a month. Faced with explosive growth in a program whose expense was shared with the federal government, other Republican governors were supporting Nixon's guaranteed-income plan, under which Washington would assume the full responsibility for welfare costs. Reagan thought the concept of a guaranteed income was ridiculous, and traveled to Washington to testify against it. His opposition helped kill Nixon's plan in the Senate and left the president fretting about a primary challenge in 1972.

Back in California, Reagan worked with Democrats to pass welfare legislation in 1971 that curtailed eligibility while raising payments to those who qualified. It also funded a test of the idea of requiring work in exchange for benefits. Although Reagan's successor, Jerry Brown, canceled the pilot program as soon as he took office, the concept behind it would return. Reagan's premise that government shouldn't subsidize freeloaders animated state-level reform initiatives over the next two decades, and ultimately led to federal legislation abolishing welfare as an entitlement in 1996.

Another priority for Reagan was tax cutting. He called a special election in 1973 to pass Proposition 1, a complicated antitax amendment to the state constitution, and lost. But the defeat laid the groundwork for Proposition 13—the 1978 initiative that put drastic limitations on property taxes while requiring a supermajority for other tax increases—and on a national level for Reagan's federal income tax cut as president in 1981.

Reagan left the Governor's Mansion in 1975 without any significant record as either a tax cutter or a budget cutter. During his time in office, California's top personal income tax rose from 7 percent to 11 percent, while the sales tax rose from 3 percent to 6 percent, the corporate tax rate went up from 5.5 percent to 9.0 percent, and the top inheritance tax rose from 10 percent to 15 percent. State revenues climbed from $2.9 billion in 1966 (the last year before Reagan took office) to $8.6 billion in 1974 (the last year for which he was responsible). In inflation-adjusted terms, state government doubled on his watch, a faster rate of growth than under his predecessor, Pat Brown, or his successor, Jerry Brown.

Reagan didn't let the reality of expanding government intrude on his belief that he was shrinking it. He'd point to the $5 billion in onetime rebates he'd given to California taxpayers—neglecting to explain that these were paid for by tax increases. But in a larger sense, Governor Reagan did block the march of liberalism. Throughout the boom years of the Great Society, he offered a coherent set of objections: social programs were wasteful and cost too much; they encouraged dependency; they diminished freedom. These arguments were steadily eroding the consensus around activist government. In 1964, the year of Reagan's first important speech, 22 percent of Americans said they didn't trust the federal government to do the right thing most of the time. By 1980, the year he was elected president, that number was 73 percent. In the intervening years, Reagan would become the most prominent face of that distrust.

6

Call It Mysticism

As his second term as governor wound down, Reagan broadened his message, returning to his favorite theme: America's place as God's chosen nation. In a speech to the first Conservative Political Action Conference (CPAC), in January 1974, he quoted John Winthrop's invocation of the community of Puritans "as a city upon a hill," an image picked up via an address of John F. Kennedy's.

> You can call it mysticism if you want to, but I have always believed that there was some divine plan that placed this great continent between two oceans to be sought out by those who were possessed of an abiding love of freedom and a special kind of courage.

Government might be failing, but Americans, he insisted, were not.

Reagan's appetite to lead was evident. But as he neared the age of sixty-five, it appeared that his political career might be over. He'd promised not to run for a third term as governor, and he wasn't interested in a Senate race. He had remained loyal to Nixon through Watergate, saying that the president should be presumed innocent and describing those after Nixon as a "lynch mob." But Gerald Ford's ascent to the presidency upon Nixon's resignation blocked Reagan's path. Preparing to leave Sacramento, he wasn't sure whether to retire to the big ranch he and Nancy had bought in the

Santa Ynez Mountains, north of Santa Barbara, or challenge Ford for the 1976 Republican nomination.

Ford's pardon of Nixon in September 1974 created an unexpected opening. The announcement dissipated the new president's initial surge of goodwill and cost him twenty points in his approval rating. In 1975 the undignified American exodus from Saigon, revelations about CIA misdeeds, and two bizarre presidential assassination attempts in seventeen days all contributed to a pervasive sense of national dishonor and disarray. "I must say to you that the state of the Union is not good," the unelected president declared in his first State of the Union address. Ford's inadequacy to the moment was captured by his impotent chirp at inflation in the form of WIN ("Whip Inflation Now") buttons.

Ford's haplessness bred discontent on the right. Battered by Watergate and the resignations of Vice President Spiro Agnew and President Nixon, the GOP lost forty-three House seats and four Senate seats in the 1974 midterm election. One of the four governorships it lost was California's, for which Reagan left no heir. After the rout, the Republican National Committee made buttons proclaiming, "Republicans Are People, Too!" Some thought the party was so discredited that it should change its name. Reagan rejected this hand-wringing. No longer checked by the need for compromise with Democrats, he shifted right, to the available spotlight. In another speech at CPAC in Washington, he declared that the GOP should raise "a banner of no pale pastels, but bold colors which make it unmistakably clear where we stand."

As with "A Time for Choosing" a decade earlier, this passionate address made Reagan a hero to conservatives, who were irked by Ford's announcement of a summit with Soviet leader Leonid Brezhnev, his amnesty for Vietnam draft dodgers, and a tax increase framed as an anti-inflation measure. Politically, Ford's worst decision was passing over Reagan in favor of Nelson Rockefeller for vice president. As rebellion brewed, Ford tried to sideline Reagan by offering to make him secretary of transportation or commerce, or ambassador to the Court of St. James's—all of which

Reagan declined. In the fall of 1975, Ford's campaign manager hinted that the president might dump Rockefeller from the ticket. Reagan was not appeased; he decried the "shoddy treatment" of the vice president, whom Ford pushed into withdrawing.

Reagan wanted to run for president, but without being seen as a politician or breaker of the Eleventh Commandment. He framed his decision around his doubts about whether Ford could win and his concern about the growth of the public sector. Claiming that 44 percent of national income went to government, he described a federal bureaucracy that had "become more intrusive, more coercive, more meddlesome and less effective." The real figure was 30 percent, but the idea that Washington was thriving at the expense of a stagnating country resonated. "In my opinion, the root of these problems lies right here—in Washington, D.C.," Reagan declared in his announcement speech at the National Press Club. "Our nation's capital has become the seat of a 'buddy' system that functions for its own benefit—increasingly insensitive to the needs of the American worker who supports it with his taxes." Reagan asserted that he was "not a member of the Washington establishment." He was "a citizen representing my fellow citizens against the institution of government."

On the campaign trail, he would tell the story of a Chicago "welfare queen" who became his emblem of the problem. "She has eighty names, thirty addresses, twelve Social Security cards and is collecting veteran's benefits on four non-existing deceased husbands. And she is collecting Social Security on her cards," he said. "She's got Medicaid, getting food stamps, and she is collecting welfare under each of her names. Her tax-free cash income is over $150,000." This story was largely accurate, but rested on a mistaken assumption. Middle-class whites who believed that federal social spending meant transferring their tax dollars to minorities thought that the welfare queen was black, as did Reagan. Linda Taylor, the person on whom this story was based, was actually white.

Where Reagan ran into trouble was on policy matters. A young aide was assigned to draft a new stump speech, which the candidate debuted before a business group in Chicago. As an alternative to the forty-year trend of transferring taxes and authority to Washington, Reagan proposed a program of "creative federalism." The federal government could save ninety billion dollars a year by turning welfare, Medicare, and food stamps over to the states. Ford's campaign developed its own analysis, suggesting the plan would raise unemployment, deepen the recession, and drive states into bankruptcy. In New Hampshire, which had no sales or income tax, the implications of the ninety-billion-dollar plan put Reagan on the defensive. A political error exacerbated the policy one. When his autocratic campaign manager, John Sears, sent him off to Illinois two days before the vote, Reagan didn't question the decision. He ended up losing the New Hampshire primary by 1,300 votes, and because his aides had been confidently raising expectations, the press counted his narrow defeat as a large one.

After the New Hampshire debacle, Reagan shifted his ground to foreign policy. Revisiting the illusory "missile gap" that John F. Kennedy had trumpeted in 1960, he charged that the United States was falling behind the Soviet Union militarily, and that Ford was accommodating the enemy instead of confronting it. "Détente, isn't that what the farmer has with the turkey until Thanksgiving Day?" he joked. Reagan held Secretary of State Henry Kissinger responsible for Ford's refusal to meet with the exiled Russian Nobel laureate Aleksandr Solzhenitsyn and for signing the Helsinki Accords, which, along with many on the right, he viewed as ratifying Soviet domination over the "captive nations" of Eastern Europe.

Ford's response of banning the word *détente* from his vocabulary was characteristic of a vacuous campaign. In one empty speech, the president boldly defended homemaking from its alleged enemies. Reagan, meanwhile, was an appealing underdog, trading in ideas that had been percolating in the pages of the *National Review* and *Commentary*. Out of money after losing in Florida, Massachusetts, and Illinois, he resurrected his campaign with another prerecorded half-hour speech that ran on fifteen North Carolina television stations. His upset victory in that state put him back in contention. Now Reagan was winning—Texas, Alabama, Georgia, Indiana, and

California. But the delegate math was daunting, and at every stop reporters asked him when he was going to drop out.

The race came down to a delegate fight in the last six weeks before the Republican convention in Kansas City. Though the primaries finished with Ford shy of the magic number 1,130, he needed the support of only 37 of 136 uncommitted delegates to secure the nomination. But as the press was on the verge of calling the race for Ford, Reagan grabbed attention back by announcing that he would select Senator Richard Schweicker of Pennsylvania as his running mate. This was both a play for uncommitted Pennsylvania delegates and a delaying tactic. Meanwhile, Reagan's allies were harrying Ford's supporters on the platform committee by proposing a "morality in foreign policy" plank that praised Solzhenitsyn and attacked the Helsinki Accords. The Reagan camp found a wily adversary, however, in Ford's young chief of staff, Dick Cheney, who had recently stepped in to fix the broken campaign. Cheney's trick for defanging Reagan's ideological attack was quietly to capitulate.

Once it became clear that Ford could not be denied the nomination, the convention turned to the question of a running mate. Reagan was the obvious, unifying choice but, playing hard-to-get, he told Sears he didn't want to be asked. Sears, not quite reading his boss, passed along the request that Ford not raise the question with Reagan. Ford chose Senator Robert Dole of Kansas instead. Being passed over only reinforced Reagan's status as the sentimental favorite at the convention. On the final night in Kansas City, Ford called him to the podium; Reagan made a flourish of resisting, and then yielded to deliver an ostensibly spontaneous address that he had privately rehearsed. Recalling a contribution he'd made to a time capsule, he wondered what the future would think about those in the room. "Will they look back with appreciation and say, 'Thank God for those people in 1976 who headed off that loss of freedom, who kept us now 100 years later free, who kept our world from nuclear destruction'?" To most of his audience, he still sounded like the Reagan of "A Time for Choosing." But the call to prevent nuclear catastrophe afforded a glimpse of a Reagan the world didn't know yet: not the Cold Warrior of 1964, but the peacemaker of 1986.

7

I Paid for That Microphone

Reagan's near miss and Ford's defeat at the hands of Jimmy Carter in the 1976 general election made Reagan the leading contender for the Republican nomination in 1980. It also left him with his pick of opportunities. He turned down an invitation to deliver conservative commentaries on the *CBS Evening News*, then the most powerful news platform in the country, on the theory that people would get tired of looking at him. Instead, he resumed the daily radio commentaries he'd begun writing after leaving Sacramento until declaring his presidential candidacy in 1975. Combined with giving speeches, this was a way for him to earn money and continue influencing the Republican Party at a time when it controlled no branch of the government. Most important, a syndicated radio presence ensured that he would remain a political force at an age when many dismissed him as too old to contend again for the presidency.

Reagan's commentaries were eventually carried on 286 stations and ran as a column in 226 newspapers across the country, reaching a combined audience of 20 million people. Well into the era of its eclipse, he grasped the persistent power of radio. Reagan understood the intimacy of the invisible human voice and the way it let listeners fill in a picture with their imaginations. His future secretary of state George Shultz recalled once having the president mark up a foreign policy speech he had written. "You've written this so it can be read. . . . That's perfectly appropriate," Reagan said to him. "But I talk to people—when they are in front of me, or at the other end of a television camera or a radio microphone—and that's different."

The handwritten drafts of those 1970s radio commentaries refute the stereotype of Reagan as an "amiable dunce." They show him to be intellectually engaged and serious-minded, if narrow in his frame of reference, which relies heavily on the conservative press. They also provide the clearest answer to the question of how Reagan moved from being a candidate of the far right to uniting the Republican Party around an ideology whose main features endure to this day. At the heart of the commentaries is Reagan's view of the "good natured, generous spirit that has been an American characteristic for as long as there has been an America" and its conflict with growing state control, represented by "the road our English cousins have already taken." Reflecting on his presidential campaign in his first commentary after the election, he notes his belief "that if government would someday quietly close the doors; if all the bureaucrats would tiptoe out of the marble halls, it would take the people of this country quite a while to miss them or even know they were gone."

Many of the commentaries concern American military vulnerability and, while cogently argued, often contain nonsense he had accumulated from right-wing sources. "Apparently the Russians have a laser beam capable of blasting our missiles from the sky if we should ever try to use them," Reagan says in a May 1977 commentary seemingly drawn from his Brass Bancroft movies. He attributes to "Nicolai" Lenin the claim that "it would not matter if ¾ of the human race perished; the important thing is that the remaining ¼ be Communist." (When I visited the Reagan Presidential Library in 2015, this quote was stenciled onto one of the walls, still a passed-along fake, but now correctly misattributed to Vladimir Ilyich Lenin.) But if Reagan discussing the Soviets sometimes sounded like Goldwater on shore leave, in one curious respect he did not. He thought it possible, as he wrote in an October 1975 commentary, "that they will see the fallacy of their way & give up their goal" or that "their system will collapse."

It's his repetition in that commentary of that word *collapse* that signals Reagan's departure from conventional right-wing thinking. Reagan saw communism as an "incompetent and ridiculous system" that ultimately couldn't withstand a full-throttled moral and military challenge from the United States. He made a hobby of collecting jokes expressing the dissatisfaction of Soviet citizens with their system. *The Commissar came to the collective farm to see how the harvest was doing and asked a farmer. The farmer said, "Oh, comrade commissar! If we took all the potatoes, they would reach the foot of God." "Comrade farmer, this is the Soviet Union. There is no God." "That's okay, there are no potatoes."* Some journalists covering Reagan's 1980 presidential campaign assumed he anticipated nuclear war with the Soviets. In fact, he envisioned an American victory without war, a view going back to his Hollywood experience of licking the Communists without getting his clothes dirty. He thought Soviet totalitarianism could be pressured to succumb in the same way.

The earliest evidence of Reagan's belief in Soviet forfeit is a statement entitled "Are Liberals Really Liberal?" typed on his personal stationery and bearing his handwritten notation "Written around 1962." After expressing skepticism that the Soviets would moderate their behavior based on American accommodation, he explained his alternative approach. "The other way is based on the belief (supported so far by all evidence) that in an all out race our system is stronger, and eventually the enemy gives up the race as a hopeless cause. Then a noble nation believing in peace extends the hand of friendship and says there is room in the world for both of us." Reagan reused exactly those words in one of his commentaries. And what might prompt the Soviets to give up? In 1977 he picked up on the story of a discontented Russian shipyard worker who wanted to bring his family to the West for a better life. "Maybe we should drop a few million typical mail order catalogs on Minsk and Pinsk and Moscow to whet their appetites," the old appliance spokesman proposed.

Reagan's optimism about the Soviets could sound naïve, which is why he kept some of his views to himself after declaring his candidacy again in November 1979. The neoconservatives he began meeting through his foreign policy adviser, Richard V. Allen, also obscured his personal opinions. Reagan cited the movement's most influential article, Jeane J. Kirkpatrick's "Dictatorships and Double Standards," which distinguished authoritarian regimes from totalitarian ones on the basis that the former, which respected property rights, could evolve toward democracy, while the latter could not. But Reagan himself believed something different: that while Communist regimes were indeed the worst, they were doomed as a violation of human nature.

And while he agreed that the United States was prosecuting the Cold War with insufficient vigor, he harbored doubts about its fundamental doctrines. Reagan didn't accept containment because he wanted to reverse Soviet domination. He doubted deterrence because he didn't believe it would keep America safe, and also because he thought the Soviets didn't believe in it. He found the concept of mutually assured destruction (MAD) both morally repugnant and absurd, comparing it to "two westerners standing in a saloon aiming their guns to each other's heads—permanently." In July 1979 he visited the North American Aerospace Defense Command (NORAD), the underground nuclear command center in Colorado. There he was dismayed to learn there was no way to defend against Soviet missiles except by launching a massive counterstrike. He left worrying that, as president, he'd have only two choices in the face of attack: "to press the button or do nothing."

What might be the alternative? In a memo following up on the visit, his aide Martin Anderson suggested pursuing a "protective missile system." Reagan liked the idea, but his military advisers wanted to keep him on the firmer ground of opposing the Anti-Ballistic Missile Treaty that Nixon had signed with Brezhnev in 1972. The logic behind the treaty was that the ability to defend missile silos against intercontinental ballistic missiles, which was largely conceptual at that point, could drive a new race to build multiple-warhead missiles able to defeat ABM systems. Reagan opposed the ABM Treaty, along with the unratified SALT II (Strategic Arms Limitations) Treaty, as reflections of a stability logic he doubted, and because of an overriding skepticism about arms control agreements in general. He frequently recommended a book by his friend Laurence Beilenson, *The Treaty Trap*, which argued that nations abide by agreements with other nations only so long as it remains in their self-interest, and that peace treaties never lead to peace.

· · ·

For the first several months, Reagan's 1980 campaign was run once again by John Sears, who insisted on full control as the price of his participation. In 1976, Reagan had been the candidate of the right, but this time Sears wanted him to be a unity candidate, which meant emphasizing President Jimmy Carter's failures rather than drawing distinctions with more moderate primary rivals such as George H. W. Bush, Howard Baker, and Bob Dole. Sears pushed out the old Sacramento loyalists he found threatening, including the two aides closest to Reagan, Ed Meese and Mike Deaver. But in the Iowa caucuses, Sears miscalculated by keeping Reagan aloof from voters and ducking a debate. After Bush won Iowa in an upset, Sears reversed tack, putting his candidate on a bus tour around New Hampshire and asking for a debate.

Reagan and Bush, the two front-runners, agreed to debate each other without the other, more marginal candidates on the Saturday before the primary. When Dole complained to the Federal Election Commission that this would constitute an illegal contribution to the two campaigns by the Nashua *Telegraph*, which was sponsoring the debate, the Reagan campaign agreed to foot the cost of the event. Sears then played a trick on Bush, inviting the four excluded candidates to show up at the event. When they all walked onto the stage, Jon Breen, the editor of the *Telegraph*, was incensed. Standing by the prior agreement, he ordered that Reagan's microphone be shut off. "I paid for this microphone, Mr. Green," Reagan testily insisted. Bush, pretending to ignore the commotion and staring straight ahead, was memorably described looking like "a small boy who has been dropped off at the wrong birthday party." Nothing else said at the debate mattered. Three days later, Reagan beat Bush by a wide margin.

But Reagan's inner circle had lost confidence in the authoritarian

Sears, who expressed blithe unconcern about the campaign's precarious finances. It was Nancy Reagan who finally stepped in to get her husband to deal with the situation. On voting day in New Hampshire, before the results came in, Reagan fired Sears and two of his close allies. Deaver and Meese were back in charge, along with a new campaign manager, William J. Casey, a Wall Street lawyer and former chairman of the Securities and Exchange Commission. In contrast to Sears, the philosophy of the old Sacramento hands was to "let Reagan be Reagan." He more or less locked up the nomination by mid-March, though Bush did not concede until late May.

Bush was the logical running mate, providing both geographic and ideological balance. But Ron and Nancy considered him whiny and, based on what they'd seen in Nashua, a poor performer under pressure. Reagan wanted former president Ford in the supporting role. He flew to Ford's golf course office in Palm Springs to sound him out. Ford couldn't get comfortable with Reagan, describing him astutely as "one of the few political leaders I have met whose public speeches revealed more than his private conversations." He told the presumptive nominee he wasn't interested. But when Ford delivered a rousing speech to the Detroit convention that seemed to indicate interest, Reagan went back to him, and Ford didn't shut the door.

Wooing Ford to join a "dream ticket," Reagan aides got carried away and stumbled into proposing a kind of copresidency. This interested Ford, but was less appealing to Reagan than sharing an office with George H. W. Bush. Reagan pulled his offer to Ford and extended one to Bush, who eagerly agreed. Reagan's acceptance speech the following night promised a balanced budget, lower taxes, and a reinvigorated military. He quoted Franklin Roosevelt's 1932 Democratic Convention pledge to reduce government and make it solvent, without any recognition of the irony that, faced with the irreconcilability of his goals, Roosevelt in office had embarked on a massive expansion of the federal government.

In September, polls showed Reagan and Carter running neck and neck. But Carter had emerged from the Democratic convention damaged by Ted Kennedy's vigorous primary challenge, much as Ford had been damaged by Reagan's in 1976. Liberals were disenchanted with Carter. Many in the center, meanwhile, were swayed by John Anderson, a liberal Republican congressman running as an independent. On the right, by contrast, an energetic movement was united behind Reagan. Neoconservatives, free-market economists from the Chicago School, and less reputable supply-siders generated a stream of ideas. Dozens of conservative publications popularized and promoted them. A new type of Washington institution turned them into policy proposals. The old model of the Washington think tank, the Brookings Institution, was neutral-liberal. The new model was activist-radical. Its avatar was the Heritage Foundation, founded in 1973 with funding from the conservative tycoons Joseph Coors and Richard Mellon Scaife.

Another component of Reagan's coalition was newly politicized southern evangelicals, who had voted mostly Democratic in previous elections. Their nominal leader was Jerry Falwell, who founded the Moral Majority in 1979. A religious revival had been gathering force, in reaction to the cultural transformations of the 1960s. Recreational drugs and sexual freedom, the pursuit of self-realization and self-expression, were still somewhat elite phenomena in the 1960s. They hit home for middle-aged and middle-class Americans in the 1970s, with an explosion in divorce rates, conflicts between parents and children, and an overwhelming sense of social disorder. Reagan spoke to an idealized vision of the time before that social revolution took hold.

Reagan's first major speech after the convention seemed to play to the worst aspect of this nostalgia. In Philadelphia, Mississippi, where three civil rights workers had been murdered in 1964, he spoke in favor of "states' rights," a term associated with segregation. Reagan prided himself on his lack of prejudice and hadn't been the one to choose the location. So when Carter accused him of bigotry, the charge backfired, making the president appear nasty. His continuing attempts to portray Reagan as a warmonger boomeranged in a similar way. Whatever harm they did to Reagan was outweighed by the damage they wrought on Carter's image of decency and restraint. The personal attacks also riled Reagan in a way that made him a better campaigner. In response, he cast the incumbent as weak and incompetent.

That shoe fit. Carter was beleaguered by the Iranian hostage crisis, an energy crisis, and a deepening recession. Over the summer, the inflation rate was 14 percent, which, combined with an unemployment rate of 8 percent, added up to a "misery index" of 22. The interest rate on thirty-year mortgages crested above 16 percent. At a moment when the country needed strong leadership, Carter mainly expressed doubt. He was uncomfortable with the ceremonial aspects of power, carrying his own luggage and banning the playing of "Hail to the Chief." He was a micromanager, a grappler with uncomfortable truths, and a confronter of unpleasant realities. On *60 Minutes*, he gave his own presidency grades of B and C on foreign, domestic, and economic policy. In a nationally televised address in July 1979 that become known as his malaise speech, Carter spoke to the nation about a crisis of confidence "that strikes at the very heart and soul and spirit of our national will" and of "the growing doubt about the meaning of our own lives."

Reagan, by contrast, believed that America's best days were ahead. "I find no national malaise. I find nothing wrong with the American people," he declared on the eve of the election. Reagan said that Carter should be reelected "if he instills in you pride for your country and a sense of optimism about our future." Reagan's confident patriotism overlooked national failings in favor of past triumphs, future opportunities, and enduring virtues. This combination of nostalgia and optimism expressed his cultivated myopia. Events that were farther away in time often seemed more real to him than those close at hand. Reagan's nostalgic nationalism led him to focus on the pending "giveaway" of the Panama Canal. "We bought it, we paid for it, it's ours, and we're going to keep it," he liked to say. Panama was ruled by a right-wing military dictatorship, not a left-wing one, but the issue expressed the idea that America was being played for a global patsy.

Reagan sometimes made trouble for himself with the antigovernment factoids he picked up in the conservative press, or in letters from his admirers. He was ridiculed for his claim that the eruption of the Mount St. Helens volcano produced more sulfur dioxide than ten years of driving; that the Occupational Safety and Health Administration had 144 regulations about climbing ladders; and that the Department of Health, Education, and Welfare spent three dollars on administration for every one dollar it gave out in payments. But at least one of his gaffes was a calculated provocation. At a Teamsters convention in Ohio, he referred to "the Carter Depression." When challenged that the country wasn't experiencing a depression, he parried, "If he wants a definition, I'll give him one. A recession is when your neighbor loses his job. A depression is when you lose yours. And recovery is when Jimmy Carter loses his."

The League of Women Voters invited all three major candidates to participate in head-to-head debates. Carter would agree to participate only if Anderson were excluded, and several of Reagan's aides thought a debate without Anderson was too risky. But after debating Anderson on his own and performing competently, Reagan agreed to a single debate with Carter, which was scheduled to be held in Cleveland, a week before Election Day. Expectations were against Reagan, which meant he only had to hold the stage to be judged the winner. In fact, Reagan's debating skill was considerable. His focus was on countering the Democratic accusation that he was dangerous. "I'm only here to tell you that I believe with all my heart that our first priority must be world peace," he said in his first answer, going on to use the word *peace* again and again.

Where Goldwater challenged a New Deal that had given hope to the country, Reagan trained his objections on later antipoverty programs that didn't serve the white middle class. He cast himself as the candidate of change, ready to abandon efforts that weren't working. He made Carter into the bureaucratic conservative trying to preserve the federal Leviathan even in places such as the desolate South Bronx, where its failures were most evident. At one point Carter pointed out, accurately, that Reagan began his political career opposing Medicare. In response, Reagan delivered one of his most memorable lines. "There you go again," he said, shaking his head. In his closing remarks, Reagan framed a question:

> Are you better off than you were four years ago? Is it easier for you to go and buy things in the stores than it was four years ago? Is there more or less unemployment in the country than there was four years ago? Is America as respected throughout the world as it was four years ago? Do you feel that our security is as safe, that we're as strong as we were four years ago?

This was his father's salesmanship, and his gift for simplification at its finest. In a wonderful Freudian slip, Carter thanked the people of Cleveland "for being such hospitable hosts during these last few hours in my life."

8

The Present Crisis

In the limousine with Carter on the way to his inauguration, Reagan did what he often did in awkward social situations: he told old Hollywood stories. When they arrived at the Capitol, the outgoing president took one of his aides aside. "Who's Jack Warner?" he wanted to know.

Reagan seemed to have the Warner Bros. era (and 1933, in particular) on his mind. Like his old idol Franklin Roosevelt, he was taking office amid crisis: a new kind of recession, a Soviet threat he analogized to the fascist one, and the hostage drama playing out in Tehran on a split screen as he was being sworn in. Dismissing the pessimism of the Carter years, Reagan told ordinary people that they were "heroes" with "every right to dream heroic dreams." What impeded those dreams was Washington.

We are a nation that has a government—not the other way around. And this makes us special among the nations of the earth. Our Government has no power except that granted it by the people. It is time to check and reverse the growth of government which shows signs of having grown beyond the consent of the governed. It is my intention to curb the size and influence of the Federal establishment and to demand recognition of the distinction between the powers granted to the Federal Government and those reserved to the states or to the people.

Or, as he put it, "In the present crisis, government is not the solution, government is the problem." Reagan wanted to end his address with a story that he'd read in a letter from a supporter about Martin Treptow, a young soldier killed in the First World War, who had written a moving pledge in his diary to sacrifice and fight "as if the whole struggle depended on me alone." The letter said that Treptow was buried in Arlington National Cemetery. But as White House speechwriters learned in their research, Treptow was buried in Bloomer, Wisconsin. Confronted with this gap, Reagan still refused to relinquish the image of a boy buried amid "the sloping hills of Arlington National Cemetery with its row upon row of simple white markers."

The style of the inaugural celebration marked a transformation in the culture of Washington. Parsimony was out. *Dynasty*, which had premiered on ABC a week earlier and would run the length of the Reagan presidency, was in. Private planes brought wealthy Republican contributors to Washington; limousines conveyed celebrities from event to event. The parties cost $19.4 million. Nancy's white, hand-beaded Galanos gown alone cost $10,000. In 1977, Carter's inaugural festivities had cost $3 million, and Rosalynn Carter recycled the gown she'd worn to her husband's swearing in as governor of Georgia. Nancy was soon ordering new china, redecorating the White House, and upgrading the menus at state dinners.

For his chief of staff, Reagan passed over Ed Meese, who had led the transition, and chose the more disciplined and effective James Baker, a Houston lawyer who was George Bush's best friend. Baker advised Reagan to devote his first three months exclusively to his economic recovery program. In his February 18 speech to a joint session of Congress, Reagan framed his plan as an urgent response to intolerable levels of unemployment, inflation, and a national debt approaching $1 trillion—or, as he translated, a stack of thousand-dollar bills sixty-seven miles high. Reagan proposed reducing Carter's proposed 1982 budget by $41.4 billion, which he claimed could be done "without harm to government's legiti-

mate purposes or to our responsibility to all who need our benev-
olence." He asked Congress for a substantial increase in military
spending, a 30 percent reduction in personal tax rates over three
years, and a reduction in the top capital gains tax rate to 20 percent.
The glaring omission from his speech, and from the accompanying
281-page blueprint, was his campaign pledge of a balanced budget
by 1983. A month in, Reagan's advisers already recognized that
this wasn't remotely compatible with his other priorities.

Reaganomics had four major components: reducing taxes, cutting domestic spending, implementing deregulation, and using
monetary policy to combat inflation. Regulatory policy would be
driven primarily at the agency level. Monetary policy was the prov-
ince of Federal Reserve chairman Paul Volcker, whom Reagan was
lucky to inherit. Reconciling his conflicting commitments around
taxes and spending fell to budget director David Stockman, a former
congressman from Michigan, who at thirty-four was the youngest
cabinet officer in 150 years. Stockman grew up on a Michigan farm
with Republican parents, and was a student leftist before turning
libertarian at Harvard Divinity School. He wanted to demonstrate
his integrity by attacking "weak claims, not weak claimants."

His contempt for Reagan's anecdotal thinking, which functioned
in a way contrary to his own analytical intelligence, was never far
from the surface. It was obvious to Stockman that Reagan's campaign promises didn't add up. This was not apparent to Reagan,
who kept telling his aides to work it out. Reagan had encountered
the same problem in Sacramento in 1967, where he eventually
agreed to increase taxes to close a budget gap. But in the White
House, he wasn't prepared to do that. Stockman couldn't get Reagan
to support budget reductions large enough to cover the cost of his
tax cuts and new weapons, or even to acknowledge the problem.

One way of closing the gap was applying the methods of supply-
side economics. Reagan's economic circle included people such
as Arthur Laffer, who believed that tax cuts would produce so much
economic growth that they would effectively pay for themselves.
During the primary campaign, George Bush had ridiculed Reagan's

support for tax cuts based on supply-side assumptions as "voodoo economic policy." But Reagan went only partway with the supply-siders. Based on his experience in Hollywood, he saw it as common sense that people would work harder if they had to pay less of what they earned to the government. But neither he nor Stockman was looking for a way to avoid cutting the budget. They wanted to cut the budget.

Some believed that Reagan's deficits were intentional. Senator Daniel Patrick Moynihan of New York, who had been a mentor to Stockman at Harvard, maintained that Reagan was trying to "starve the beast," using deficits to force cuts in domestic spending. In a 1981 address from the Oval Office, Reagan said, "We can lecture our children until we are out of voice and breath. Or we can cure their extravagance by simply reducing their allowance." But Stockman always denied that the deficits were a cynical strategy to force budget cuts. He believed that Reagan simply turned away from recognizing the existence of trade-offs.

The budget chief grew increasingly frustrated as he was checked at every pass. Reagan's goal was to shrink government to something more like what it was before the 1960s. "The press is dying to paint me as now trying to undo the New Deal," he wrote in his diary. "I remind them I voted for F.D.R. 4 times. I'm trying to undo the 'Great Society.' It was L.B.J.'s war on poverty that led to our present mess." Even so, Reagan took off the table, for the first year, cuts not just in Social Security but also in Medicare and Medicaid, which were Great Society programs. Then he turned those exemptions into an indefinite promise.

Because these entitlements consumed some 60 percent of federal spending, the only other place to look for savings was in military spending. But Caspar Weinberger, Reagan's secretary of defense, knew him well going back to his days working for him in Sacramento, and understood the federal budget from his time in Stockman's job under Nixon. Weinberger trapped the president into backing a 7 percent increase in military spending based not on Carter's 1980 budget of $142 billion, but off of a congressional baseline that had already risen by almost 50 percent, to $222 billion. This was a huge bank error in his favor, but Weinberger refused to yield any portion of it. Taking advantage of Reagan's aversion to conflict, he refused any compromise with Stockman.

In the end, Stockman dealt with overspending through what he called his magic asterisk: "future savings to be identified." This was code for surrendering to deficits. While proposing meaningful cuts in food stamps and a variety of other domestic programs, Reagan's 1982 budget proposed increasing overall federal spending by 11.2 percent. Both the president and his opponents had a stake in portraying his domestic budget cuts as much bigger than they were. Congressional Democrats, who wanted to attack Reagan for his savage attacks on the poor, helped convince the president that he really was proposing "the greatest attempt of savings in the history of the nation."

• • •

On March 30, Reagan had just finished touting his economic plan in a lunch speech to the carpenters' section of the AFL-CIO at the Washington Hilton. As he was getting into his limousine, gunshots were fired. Only after shoving him into the car and peeling away did Secret Service agents realize he'd been shot, struck in the chest by a ricochet off the door. They rushed him to George Washington University Hospital. Despite great pain and difficulty breathing, Reagan insisted on walking through the front entrance to the emergency room. Inside, he collapsed to the floor.

As soon as he regained consciousness, the president began making jokes. To the nurse attending to him: "Who's holding my hand? Does Nancy know about us?" To Nancy a few minutes later: "Honey, I forgot to duck." To the surgeon about to operate: "I hope you're a Republican." Reagan's doctors played their expected part in the deception that the president's life was never at risk and that he was quickly his usual self again following surgery. After meeting with Lyn Nofziger, a White House official, Dennis O'Leary, the doctor in charge of briefing the press, baldly lied: "The President's vital signs were absolutely rock stable through this whole thing. . . . He was at no time in any serious danger." O'Leary said the president would be able to put in a full day of work so long as he got a nap. In fact, Reagan had narrowly escaped death, losing half the blood in his body. Disoriented, and with a breathing tube in his throat, he wrote that night, "[W]here am I?" He subsequently developed a high fever and pneumonia, which was also kept from the press. He lost twelve pounds in as many days in the hospital.

"Why did he do it? What's his beef?" Reagan scrawled on a pad that first night, when he was still on a respirator and unable to speak. The attempted assassin was John Hinckley, a college student from Texas who had arrived the day before on a Greyhound bus with a .22 handgun he'd bought for forty-seven dollars at a Dallas pawnshop. Hinckley had been stalking the actress Jodie Foster and was playing out a demented attempt to impress her by shooting Reagan.

Reagan scribbled other notes that first night. "Will I be able to ride my horses again? Will I be able to cut brush?" He would ride again, but he carried deficits from his injuries. Reagan had long been hard of hearing on his right side, the result of a blank being fired too near his ear during the filming of *Secret Service of the Air*. Now, as Nancy told their daughter Patti, it was worse. Ron Jr. noticed his father slowing down, speaking less, and making less of an effort to remember who people were. At a reception for big-city mayors not long after the assassination attempt, Reagan greeted his secretary of housing and urban development, Samuel Pierce, who was the only black member of his cabinet, "How are you, Mr. Mayor? How are things in your city?"

Events of that day would have a permanent effect on Reagan's presidency. His press secretary, James Brady, was shot in the head and would never fully recover. Chief of Staff James Baker was reluctant to invoke the Twenty-Fifth Amendment and make his close friend Vice President Bush the acting president while Reagan was incapacitated, as he ought to have done. Baker was concerned that the right wing, which didn't trust them, "might view the transfer as something just short of a Bush-Baker *coup d'état*." This mistake created a dangerous authority vacuum. With Brady's deputy Larry Speakes floundering in the White House

Briefing Room, Secretary of State Alexander Haig ran up and grabbed the lectern. "As of now, I am in control here, in the White House, pending the return of the vice president." It sounded almost as if the transparently ambitious former general was declaring a military coup. His reputation would never recover. Reagan himself faced heavier restrictions from the Secret Service, which kept him from public appearances in open venues and forced him to wear what he called an "iron t-shirt." Security concerns now prevented him from attending church on Sundays, or gave him an excuse not to do so.

Once home from the hospital, Reagan was as politically enhanced as he was physically attenuated. His grace in extremis had changed the way he was seen by the public. By early April, his approval rating had surged to 67 percent. His speech to a joint session of Congress that month had Democrats standing and applauding alongside Republicans. "That reception was almost worth getting shot," Reagan joked. He recognized his new latitude. He used his limited energy to line up votes for his economic plan. At first, he focused on corralling liberal Republicans from the Northeast who might be vulnerable if they voted for his budget cuts. Next, he courted Democrats with invitations to the White House and, in some cases, promises not to campaign against them if they voted with him.

The Speaker of the House, the Boston Irish politician Tip O'Neill, recognized the new reality: "The President has become a hero. We can't argue with a man as popular as he is." At the end of June, Congress passed Reagan's budget bill. A month later, the House approved a modified version of his tax bill with 48 Democratic votes, and the Senate soon followed with an 89–11 vote. Reagan signed the tax bill into law on August 13, on the porch at his ranch. The budget included $39 billion in cuts in domestic spending, which pushed 400,000 people off the welfare rolls and reduced benefits to a further 279,000. A million people lost food stamps.

Given that these cuts took effect after the onset of the 1982 recession, when unemployment reached its highest rate since the

Great Depression, their impact was especially severe. Democrats lashed out at the president as cruel and uncaring, a Robin Hood in reverse. Their favorite illustration was the Department of Agriculture's reclassifying ketchup as a vegetable to make school lunches cheaper. Nancy's society friends and designer gowns were frequent targets as well. But most of the arrows sailed past Reagan, because they didn't match the man people saw and heard. He responded to the poor as individuals, not as a category. Throughout his presidency, he spent a significant amount of time, sometimes hours a day, reading and answering his mail, something he considered an obligation since his Hollywood days. When people wrote him about being in need, his response often included a personal check. Religiously motivated charity, the kind his mother practiced even when she herself was poor, was his alternative to public assistance. He thought people who needed help would find it through the country's "deep spirit of generosity."

Nor was Reagan antilabor, often pointing out that he had served as president of a union. He did, however, have a strong view going back to his Sacramento days that public employees had no right to strike because of their responsibility for public order and safety. This policy admitted of no exceptions, even for a union such as the Professional Air Traffic Controllers Organization, which had endorsed him in 1980. After this union rejected a Department of Transportation offer of a new contract, its president called an illegal strike. Reagan said that the air traffic controllers were violating their oath of employment and gave them forty-eight hours to return to their jobs. When they didn't, he fired eleven thousand of them, more than half of PATCO's membership, replacing them with military personnel. Despite mass flight cancellations, standing up to a lawbreaking union turned out to be a wildly popular stance.

Reagan showed his willingness to face down the right as well. When he interviewed an Arizona state judge named Sandra Day O'Connor to fill the opening left by Potter Stewart's retirement from the Supreme Court, she was clear with him: although she personally opposed abortion, *Roe v. Wade* was the law of the land. Reagan's tuning out this crucial nuance was another example of his constructive obliviousness, since appointing a more conservative justice would have risked reversing *Roe* and igniting an all-consuming national battle over abortion. His decision made, he brooked no opposition from evangelicals and other conservatives who read O'Connor accurately as someone who wouldn't vote to reverse *Roe*. He slapped down a brewing rebellion by Jerry Falwell, telling the minister to "trust my judgment on this one."

The budget was a more serious challenge. Stockman had been economical with the truth—inside the White House, to placate Reagan; outside, to avoid putting his tax cut in jeopardy. Now that the plan was law, Stockman told the president that instead of the deficit tapering to zero by 1984, it would rise from $60 billion in 1982 to $112 billion by 1986. And those numbers would hold only in the unlikely event that all the budget cuts took effect. Faced with Stockman's insistence that something had to give, Reagan chose . . . nothing. He wouldn't modify his defense increases. He wouldn't consider cutting Social Security. He wouldn't delay his tax cuts. Reagan's only suggestion was that his budget director find more savings from waste, fraud, and abuse.

Stockman finally got the president's attention after the publication of a fifty-page *Atlantic Monthly* article entitled "The Education of David Stockman." In it, the journalist William Greider recounted regular breakfasts at which the budget chief talked into a tape recorder about the administration's fiscal plan. Stockman described the underlying policy as "trickle-down economics" and acknowledged that the numbers added up only under a "rosy scenario" of 5 percent annual GDP growth. Washington demanded Stockman's head for speaking openly to a journalist. "If true, David is a turncoat," Reagan wrote in his diary, "but in reality he was victimized by what he'd always thought was a good friend." Over lunch, the president characteristically absolved him.

By the end of his first year, Stockman's message that something had to be done began to penetrate the presidential fog. "We who were going to balance the budget face the biggest deficits ever," Reagan noted in his diary on December 8. For his second budget, he agreed to propose $37.5 billion in "revenue enhancements," ducking behind obfuscatory language. "To even refer to this as a tax increase, I think was wrong," he said in signing the largest tax increase in history after it passed in 1982. "It was an adjustment to the tax cut last year." Accommodating fiscal and political realities without acknowledging them became a hallmark of the Reagan presidency. As the deficit worsened, he agreed to many more tax increases: a five-cent gas tax, followed by a hike in Social Security taxes recommended by the bipartisan Greenspan Commission. In 1984 he agreed to another $18 billion in increased taxes on phone service, liquor, and tobacco. There were further tax increases in bills Reagan signed in 1985, 1986, 1987, and 1988.

. . .

Reagan's second year began with his most radical proposal to remake the liberal state. In his State of the Union address in January 1982, Reagan advanced something called "The New Federalism," a proposal to hand over welfare and food stamps to the states in exchange for the federal government taking on full responsibility for the shared costs of Medicaid. As the grandiose phrasing suggested, it was meant as a play for the history books, and as an unmaking of the Great Society. However, the New Federalism attracted little support from governors or members of Congress in either party, and it soon faded away.

The year went downhill from there, as the recession that began in the second half of 1981 kicked in. Federal Reserve chairman Paul Volcker, a principled, cigar-chomping bear of a man, would provide no relief. He was intent on keeping interest rates high for as long as necessary to break the back of inflation. The news was now filled with stories about bank failures and farm foreclosures. The child poverty rate was on its way from 16 to 20 percent. Homelessness was a new epidemic; food pantries and soup kitchens were doing a record business. As the recession deepened and deficit projections worsened, the Dow Jones Industrial Average fell more than 20 percent, to less than 800 points in August 1982.

As the unemployment rate rose, Reagan's approval rating fell month by month, from a peak of 68 percent in May 1981 to

35 percent in January 1983. To address the burgeoning deficit, he proposed another round of reductions in Medicaid, food stamps, and welfare that were both totally inadequate to the budgetary problem he had created and, in the context of the recession, cruel. With members of his own party now running for cover, he got only a quarter of the cuts he asked for. In the months before the 1982 midterm election, the unemployment rate peaked at 10.8 percent. While Republicans managed to retain control of the Senate, Democrats added twenty-seven seats to their House majority.

Did Reagan understand what was going on with his budget and the economy? The evidence of his diaries suggests he thought about economic issues in the same segmented way he talked about them. Taxes triggered one set of views, defense another, deficits a third. This compartmentalization allowed him to deal with the reality of the economy without having to reconcile his ideology and practical necessity. When conservative principle and principled conservatives such as Stockman became an obstacle to the best available solution, Reagan didn't modify his philosophy; he simply suspended it temporarily. In his diaries, he continually dismisses Stockman's projections as too pessimistic and blames the deficit on Congress rejecting his budget cuts—never acknowledging that even his proposed cuts were wildly insufficient to the problem. He consistently made a default choice of increasing the deficit over tax increases or limiting military spending, which he regarded as "not a budget issue."

Failing to put those pieces together was Reagan's obliviousness at its most functional, allowing him to live with large deficits and a growing debt that violated his commitments but were the right political and policy choice under the circumstances. The president regarded himself as an antagonist of John Maynard Keynes, based on his understanding that Keynes was the favored economist of liberals. But in fact Reagan's deficit spending and tax cuts were Keynesianism with a right-wing skew: fiscal stimulation of the economy as it slid into recession, at a time when monetary policy could not respond in the normal way because of inflation. Putting money in the hands of working people might have been more equitable and efficient. But cutting taxes for the upper middle class and the wealthy while spurring employment at defense contractors served the same purpose.

Reagan's Keynesian borrow-and-spend policy was a wiser choice than what most of the experts around him were advocating. Wartime experience showed that the country could sustain large deficits for many years. Stockman's preference, by contrast, would have been economically and politically disastrous. Cutting toward balance in 1981 and 1982 would have deepened the recession and made it hard for the economy to recover by the 1984 election. Absent Volcker's tight monetary policy, Reagan's huge 1981 stimulus would have aggravated inflation and prevented the recovery that began in late 1982 and gathered steam through 1983 and 1984. But thanks to Volcker, inflation dropped from 14 percent in 1980 to just over 3 percent by the end of 1983, when Reagan reappointed Volcker to a second four-year term. As inflation fell, monetary policy eased, working in concert with Reagan's deficit spending and renewed business confidence to produce a period of economic expansion that lasted until 1990.

As the economy bounced back, government expanded with it. Over Reagan's two terms, domestic spending went from $303 billion to $565 billion in nominal terms. Overall federal spending rose from $671 billion in 1981 to $1.144 trillion in 1989. Since inflation accounts for most of that increase, a better measure is the federal civilian workforce, which grew by around 5 percent during the Reagan years. What Reagan did legitimately reduce was income taxes, from a top rate of 70 percent when he took office to 28 percent when he left. Although many other taxes, such as Social Security, rose to compensate, the decline in federal revenue caused the national debt to balloon from $998 billion in 1981 to $2.857 trillion in 1989. In 1983 the deficit would reach $208 billion, an alarming 5.9 percent of GDP.

Despite these numbers, Reagan believed, just as he did in California, that he was making the government smaller. The deficit, he felt, was the product of Congress's unwillingness to pass his spending cuts. In fact, Reagan didn't succeed in eliminating a single major program, which illustrates the truth of his adage about eternal life and government bureaus. What he did change was the nation's *attitude* about government, stoking its newfound unpopularity and diminishing expectations about what it was capable of doing. Reagan took citizens who a generation before had turned to Washington for solutions and told them to look elsewhere: to voluntarism, to the free market, to themselves.

9

I Think I Made a Friend

By early 1982, Reagan had set the mold for his presidency—and a new model for the presidency itself. In contrast to his recent predecessors, his focus was largely external. He devoted himself to the public, ceremonial, symbolic aspects of his job and much less to the internal, deliberative ones. For the most part, his presidency worked the way his governorship had: the president set direction and made major decisions while leaving implementation to others. The effectiveness of this management style in his first term rebutted the evidence supplied by Johnson, Nixon, Ford, and Carter that the American presidency had become an impossible job. With his confident turnaround of the biggest failing institution of them all, Reagan became the paradigm of the new CEO superman.

The biographer Richard Reeves describes Reagan as "staff-dependent" rather than "staff-driven." The staff he depended on through most of his first term was the "troika": James Baker, Michael Deaver, and Edwin Meese. The three met with him every morning and at the end of every afternoon. Baker held primary responsibility for White House operations, including the appointments process and relations with Congress, the press, the party, governors, and mayors. Deaver looked after the president himself—his schedule, his family, and his public image. Meese led on policy and coordinated relations with the cabinet.

Having set up an effective structure, Reagan tuned it out. His White House diaries, which run to five handwritten volumes, give a numbingly detailed day-by-day account of the presidency as he experienced it. The abridged published version logs eighty haircuts, twenty-one dental visits, and thirty-four allergy shots, along with countless meals, films, and horseback rides (often describing horses more feelingly than people). But in entries covering the first term, Reagan mentions only ten official meetings that include Baker, three with Meese, and two with Deaver. The president sees himself in command, with aides functioning as a transparent layer between him and the nation. He is the one who chooses O'Connor for the Supreme Court in 1981, with no mention of where he got the idea. Staff work, like stage mechanics, stays invisible. The exceptions are when aides bring Reagan an internal conflict that only he can resolve, such as the troika's insistence on getting rid of the domineering Al Haig, or when they themselves become the news, as with Stockman's self-aggrandizing act of sabotage.

To those working for him, the reality was far different. The first memoirs to emerge from the administration, Stockman's and that of Donald Regan, the president's first treasury secretary and second chief of staff, depict an intellectually detached president guided by staff to an unprecedented degree. Stockman describes Caspar Weinberger briefing Reagan with a pictogram representing levels of Pentagon funding: an unarmed midget representing Carter's, a "four-eyed wimp who looked like Woody Allen" as Stockman's, and a fully equipped GI Joe as the level Weinberger wanted. "It was so intellectually disreputable, so demeaning, that I could hardly bring myself to believe that a Harvard-educated cabinet officer could have brought this to the President of the United States," Stockman writes. Regan portrays a White House ordered around Nancy's consultations with Joan Quigley, a fashionable Hollywood astrologer. Published toward the end of Reagan's second term, when the president's engagement with detail had greatly declined from an already low threshold, these disappointed accounts tend to exaggerate the role of staff just as Reagan's diaries understate it.

Delegating the mechanics of administration and decision making to a highly empowered staff offered Reagan tremendous advantages. At a personal level, it allowed him to maintain his equilibrium and continue the kind of life he wanted to lead. In the diaries, he relishes his weekends at Camp David swimming, riding, hiking, and watching movies with Nancy. He enjoys films except when they violate his moral standards, such as *Nine to Five* (pot smoking) or *An Officer and a Gentleman* ("good story spoiled by nudity, language & sex"). He and Nancy maintain an active social life with old friends: Christmas Day with their friends the Wicks, New Year's Eve at the Annenbergs at their Sunnylands estate near Palm Springs, and White House dinners with performances by entertainer friends such as Frank Sinatra, Mel Tormé, Tony Bennett, and Burt Bacharach. He yearns for his ranch, where he spends days "exterior decorating," clearing brush and chopping up dead trees. He dreads Mondays at the office and relishes opportunities to sleep late.

At a political level, Reagan's detached management style served to diffuse accountability. Though he complained about leaking, Reagan made little effort to discourage staff from seeking attention or cultivating relationships with the media. His top aides regularly provided reporters with behind-the-scenes accounts that highlighted their own leading roles. As a result, a tacit consensus formed in Washington absolving Reagan of responsibility for the particulars of his policies. Stockman became the lightning rod for harsh budget cuts, Weinberger for excesses in military spending, interior secretary James Watt for tree cutting, and so on. To be sure, Reagan had ultimate responsibility, but everyone understood that he didn't make most decisions personally.

This sense of remove was especially useful in his handling of ideological conservatives. After the failure of his 1982 New Federalism proposal, Reagan turned more conflict averse in domestic policy. He shunned showdowns with Democrats on controversial issues such as affirmative action, school prayer, and abortion. Frustrated New Right leaders such as Howard Phillips and Paul Weyrich blamed his deviation from orthodoxy on his staff, and on Baker in particular. Their rallying cry became the slogan of John Sears's antagonists inside Reagan's 1980 primary campaign,

"Let Reagan Be Reagan"—as if the real one had somehow become a prisoner of his aides.

In fact, Reagan's tendency toward greater moderation after his first year did owe something to Baker, an establishment Republican whose moderate views were closer to those of Vice President Bush. Faced with the real-world problem of compromising on budgets with a less quiescent Democratic Congress, Baker shrewdly let divisive proposals such as abolishing the Department of Education or amending the Constitution to ban abortion fall by the wayside. Sanding the sharper edges off Reagan was hardly a perversion of the president's wishes, however. It reflected the way he had governed in California, and the level of conflict he was prepared to take on. On social policy, Reagan often preferred to express his critical views and live with the status quo. James Baker's successors, Don Regan, who came from Wall Street, and Howard Baker Jr., who came from the Senate, understood this dynamic and followed suit.

Broad delegation created the space Reagan needed to focus on his storytelling role. Writing was an activity that came naturally to him and one he was reluctant to give up or hand off after he was elected. In the White House, he still wrote out many of his Saturday radio addresses in longhand. Where others took first crack, Reagan's edits sometimes look like heavily marked English papers. He invariably improved his speechwriters' drafts with more vivid and colloquial language, a superior sense of humor, and his humanizing anecdotes. No one else could fully capture Reagan's distinctive voice. When you read what Reagan put effort into writing himself, you hear him saying it.

But storytelling for Reagan was more than just writing; it was a way of fusing himself with public narrative, often by pinning literal or figurative ribbons on crime-stopping heroes and good samaritans. In his diary, Reagan records affecting daily dramas, turning them into what might have been capsule treatments for *General Electric Theater*: "2 heroic pilots who safely landed their plane saving their passengers even though they themselves were on fire" . . . "An 18 year old went down a pipe into a tank to try to save 2 paramedics who had passed out from noxious fumes. I had to give the medal to his parents." The president can't resist playing the *deus ex machina*. Shortly before Christmas 1982, he read in the paper about an unemployed man who was on his way home from a job interview when he saw a blind man fall between two subway cars. "Young Mr. Andrews without hesitation leaped off the subway platform between the cars & rescued him," Reagan writes. "I called him—from his voice I knew he was black. I asked if he'd gotten the job . . . I called the company—the operator said the manager & his mother were both on the phone. I asked if they'd read the story—they had. Andrews has a job."

In his first State of the Union address, in 1982, Reagan brought the room to its feet when he pointed out a man sitting next to Nancy in the gallery. It was Lenny Skutnik, a printer at the Congressional Budget Office who, a week earlier, had jumped into the Potomac River to rescue one of the few survivors of a plane crash. "Just two weeks ago, in the midst of a terrible tragedy on the Potomac, we saw again the spirit of American heroism at its finest—the heroism of dedicated rescue workers saving crash victims from icy waters," Reagan said. "And we saw the heroism of one of our young Government employees, Lenny Skutnik, who, when he saw a woman lose her grip on the helicopter line, dived into the water and dragged her to safety." Calling out heroes in the gallery has been a feature of State of the Union addresses ever since, but no subsequent president has invested himself in their stories the way Reagan did.

Another story line Reagan loved was the one in which a reasonable president persuades an opponent to see things his way. In his diary, he records receiving a telegram from a woman in Peoria, Illinois, who said she wouldn't vote for him.

She was referring to abortion & she called herself an ex-Repub. who wouldn't vote for me. I was going to write her & then on a hunch I phoned. It took a little doing to convince her it was really me. We had a nice talk & I was right that her problem was abortion. I made my pitch that there were 2 people's rights involved in abortion—the mother & the unborn child. She promised to give that some deep thought. We had a nice visit. She's a 51 year old divorcee working for less than $10,000 a year—has a 17 year old son ready for college & a married daughter. I think I made a friend.

The way he tries to persuade a working mom in Illinois is essentially what he tried to do with other people who had the wrong idea about him: liberal journalists, Democratic members of Congress, and a succession of Soviet leaders. Reading late in his presidency that Thurgood Marshall had attacked his civil rights record in an interview, he invited the Supreme Court justice to the White House: "I literally told him my life story & how there was not a prejudice in me. I have examples of my relation with Minorities as a young man in school, as a sports announcer & as Gov. I think I made a friend."

. . .

The disadvantages of Reagan's style of governing were a drifting from his goals in cases where his top aides didn't fully share his commitments, the potential for error in areas where his understanding was limited, and abuses by members of his administration who weren't being watched. The first problem manifested itself in Reagan's scant accomplishments in social and domestic policy beyond his original economic program. By the 1982 midterm election, many of his Sacramento loyalists were gone, and Meese was fading in authority relative to Baker. Deaver and his ally Nancy Reagan were zealous about the president's image, not his ideology. They agreed about where the movement conservatives belonged: in the speechwriting office, where they could sound off without consequence.

Changes in personnel diminished the administration's ambitions in a way that Reagan didn't seem to notice. For him, reversing the Great Society meant reducing the federal government's role and letting people succeed or fail on their own. But after his New Federalism proposal stagnated, he had no blueprint for how to accomplish this shift. The policy battleground moved to the agencies, where Reagan wasn't engaged and where Congress held much greater sway. The president's antiregulatory drive petered out around the same time. In environmental and consumer affairs, and in food and drug safety, Reagan put deregulators in charge. But rather than attempt broad regulatory repeal, the administration went after enforcement budgets and made the process for approving new regulations more difficult. These efforts halved the thickness of the *Federal Register*, which compiles new regulations, but had a mostly passive impact in the form of weakened enforcement.

In areas such as tax cuts, defense spending, and relations with the Soviets, where Reagan expressed clear views, his subordinates generally tried to carry out some version of his wishes. In areas where his framework had less applicability, he often got into trouble. He largely missed the transformation of China, because his entire relationship to the subject revolved around maintaining support for Taiwan. His only contribution to an NSC meeting on the subject in 1983 was "You mean our position should be, 'no tickee, no laundry'?" Reagan stood by the apartheid regime in South Africa on the presumption that the African National Congress would turn the country into a Soviet satellite. The most dangerous expression of his oversimplification was in the Middle East, where he traced all terrorism to the Soviet Union. He viewed the Libyan leader Muammar Gaddafi, with whom he skirmished for eight years, as a Soviet proxy. He sent U.S. Marines to Beirut, where they became a sitting target, because he misunderstood Lebanon as a battleground of East-West conflict.

By mocking bureaucrats, undermining regulation, and paying minimal attention to government ethics, Reagan widened opportunities for abuse. The most expensive disasters took place years later, in areas of partial transition from regulation to free enterprise. In 1982, for example, Reagan signed the Garn–St. Germain Depository Institutions Act, which let savings and loans take huge risks with deposits while keeping them federally insured. The heedless dismantling of long-standing rules would lead to the collapse of hundreds of financial institutions during George H. W. Bush's presidency, necessitating a $130 billion bailout.

In areas where Reagan rejected a role for the federal government, supporters and nominees saw opportunities to plunder it. Congress's successful defense of public housing from Reagan's proposed cuts left the Department of Housing and Urban Development as a backwater implementing programs the administration didn't believe in. Samuel Pierce, the cabinet member Reagan failed to recognize at a reception for mayors, took the signal. While he watched soap operas in his office and traveled the world on junkets, his aides steered grants to politically connected developers and lobbyists, or to one another. The only cabinet member to serve the entire eight years of Reagan's term, Pierce was never indicted. But seventeen of his aides were eventually convicted, including Deborah Gore Dean, his executive assistant, on counts of defrauding the government, bribery, and lying to Congress. Pierce's successor in the Bush administration, Jack Kemp, sponsored a review that found fraud, theft, mismanagement, or influence peddling in 94 percent of HUD's budget, with costs to the government mounting into billions of dollars.

Those convicted included the former secretary of the interior James Watt, who became a lobbyist after being forced to resign in 1983 following comments he made about affirmative action, when he described a coal-leasing panel he appointed as "a black, a woman, two Jews and a cripple." Watt was the Reagan administration at its worst, combining in equal measure sleaziness, religious faux piety, and hostility to government's established role in his field. At the Interior Department, his only concern was facilitating the development of public land for profit. "We will mine more, drill more, cut more timber," he asserted. As a lobbyist, he profited from the exploitation of public resources. As part of his work, he was paid hundreds of thousands of dollars to help secure HUD contracts; he was eventually indicted on twenty-five counts of perjury and obstruction of justice. Watt agreed to plead guilty to a single count and avoided prison.

It became hard to keep track of all the congressional panels, special counsels, and independent prosecutors whose work dragged on for many years after Reagan left office. Perhaps the most illustrative scandal was Wedtech, which captured multiple aspects of the zeitgeist. The protagonist was John Mariotta, whom Reagan, with more truth than he knew, called a "hero for the eighties." Mariotta saw that the Pentagon was where the money was, so he turned his baby carriage factory into a defense contractor. He saw that Republicans wanted to lionize minority entrepreneurs creating jobs amid urban decay, so he emphasized his Puerto Rican heritage and his plant's location in the Bronx. And he saw that influence was for sale in Washington, so he hired Reagan's former aide Lyn Nofziger to lobby the Pentagon's public liaison officer Elizabeth Dole and secure a $32 million no-bid contract to make engines for the army. He also hired a San Francisco lawyer named E. Robert Wallach to enlist Ed Meese, Wallach's best friend from high school, in getting him contracts worth a quarter of a billion dollars. During Reagan's second term, twenty politicians would be convicted of bribery, perjury, and other crimes in connection with the Wedtech scandal. Meese, by then the attorney general, escaped indictment, but the furor led to his resignation.

10

The Ash Heap of History

At Reagan's first presidential press conference, Sam Donaldson of ABC News asked him about the Soviet Union's long-term intentions. The president responded that the Soviets remained dedicated to world revolution. "The only morality they recognize is what will further their cause, meaning they reserve unto themselves the right to commit any crime, to lie, to cheat, in order to attain that," Reagan said. "I think when you do business with them . . . you keep that in mind."

The reference to the right to lie and cheat came from the "Ten Commandments of Nikolai Lenin," which was also the source of Reagan's earlier bogus quote about it being acceptable for three-quarters of humanity to perish. There was, of course, no Nikolai Lenin, only a Vladimir Ilyich Lenin, who signed some of his early writings with the pseudonym "N. Lenin." Reagan's source was probably a pamphlet given to him by a California friend, distributed by the John Birch Society, and drawn from an earlier Nazi fabrication. "Not one of those quotes is genuine," Georgi Arbatov, the head of the Soviet Institute for U.S. and Canadian Studies, later complained about Reagan's frequent Lenin citations. "We are under the impression that someone is supplying these false quotations that he is using."

Reagan was no scholar. But the crudeness of his evidence supported the simplicity of his understanding. The United States faced an implacable foe that could be dealt with only from a position of strength. During his campaign, he had fastened on to the phrase "window of vulnerability," which Alexander Haig and others used to refer to the risk that the Soviets could gain a strategic edge if the United States didn't act to maintain the nuclear balance. The hawks worried that Soviet ICBMs could theoretically destroy most of America's ICBMs in their fixed silos in a first strike. To close that window, they advocated a system of MX missiles moving on underground tracks—a "survivable basing mode," in the favored jargon. Reagan misunderstood the phrase to mean that "the Soviet Union does have a definite margin of superiority."

It wasn't clear that the advisers closest to Reagan understood the distinction any better than he did. In 1981, Ed Meese was given a seat on the National Security Council and William Clark was barely confirmed as deputy secretary of state after acknowledging he knew essentially nothing about international affairs. These were Reagan's foreign policy gatekeepers. But the Sacramento alumni found common ground with the more sophisticated neoconservatives around him on the central point: he must reject any accommodation with the Soviets. The Reagan administration intended to replace détente with a policy of military dominance. The top-secret but promptly leaked Defense Planning Guidance that the president approved in March 1982 laid out his new military strategy. "Should deterrence fail and strategic nuclear war with the U.S.S.R. occur, the United States must prevail and be able to force the Soviet Union to seek earliest termination of hostilities on terms favorable to the United States," it read. The administration intended to challenge the Soviets by expanding covert and counterinsurgency operations in Latin America, Africa, and elsewhere.

The right regarded the new policy as tough but sound. The left read it as bellicose and dangerous. But both hawks and doves misunderstood Reagan's view of the Soviets, cherry-picking his remarks to make him seem more conventional while tuning out the things he sometimes said that didn't match their expectations. The big misunderstanding on the left was that Reagan thought that war with the Soviets was winnable. In fact, Reagan held the more exotic view that a combination of military, economic, and moral pressure could crumble the Soviet empire. Reagan wanted to "force them to the bargaining table," as he put it during the 1980 campaign. "They cannot vastly increase their military productivity because they've already got their people on a starvation diet," he said in October 1981. "If we show them [we have] the will and determination to go forward with a military buildup . . . they then have to weigh, do they want to meet us realistically on a program of disarmament or do they want to face a legitimate arms race in which we're racing."

Reagan's thinking about the Soviets had a crude cunning that ran parallel to his economic program, where he thought he might force Congress to shrink government by "taking away its allowance." He hoped to reverse the nuclear arms race by escalating it beyond what the Soviet system could afford. The leaked defense guidance expressed this idea by calling for the development of new high-tech weapons that would "impose disproportionate costs, open up new areas of major military competition and obsolesce previous Soviet investment." It specifically mentioned space-based weapons systems. The guidance also stated that trade policies should put maximum pressure on a Soviet economy reeling under the weight of excessive military spending. Reagan put this more bluntly to Senate majority leader Howard Baker in 1982: "What I want is to bring them to their knees so that they will disarm and let us disarm. But we have got to do it by keeping the heat on. We can do it. We have them on the ropes economically. They are selling rat meat in the markets in Russia today."

But if arming your way to disarmament wasn't necessarily a contradiction, Reagan's desire to begin negotiating a nuclear truce before his military buildup even started was. And if Communists were fundamentally untrustworthy in the way "Nikolai Lenin" pronounced that they were, how could negotiating treaties with the Soviets ever make sense? The daily expressions of Reagan's long-term strategies—inveighing against deficits while creating them, aspiring to eliminate nuclear missiles while increasing them—were often inconsistent. Failure to choose between opposing alternatives sometimes produced a zigzag pattern in his presidency. But a tolerance for cognitive dissonance, like other forms of irrationality, can be an effective negotiating tactic. The Soviets, like Tip O'Neill, were never quite sure which Reagan they were bargaining with. His ability to live with contradictions was, on balance, more blessing than curse.

After the fall of the Berlin Wall, many people remembered having had views similar to Reagan's about the vulnerability of the Soviet Union. But Reagan, as Robert Gates wrote in his 1996 memoir *From the Shadows*, "nearly alone truly believed in 1981 that the Soviet system was vulnerable not in some vague, long-range historical sense, but right then." Reagan's commonsense view of historical inevitability was that an unworkable government was sure to break down sooner or later. "Communism is neither an economic or a political system—it is a form of insanity—a temporary aberration which will one day disappear from the earth because it is contrary to human nature," he wrote in his unpublished 1962 statement, "Are Liberals Really Liberal?"

Reagan's anticipation of communism's collapse contradicted the worldview of neoconservatives he appointed to key positions guiding Cold War strategy. His ambassador to the United Nations, Jeane Kirkpatrick, contended that the Soviet Union could not change. Other neoconservatives who joined the administration shared her view of communism as irreversible. Reagan saw no need to challenge them. He had no taste for internal debates, especially theoretical ones with little bearing on policy. And since he shared their fundamental distrust of arms control, it didn't make much difference that the neoconservative goal was Soviet behavior modification whereas his was Communist downfall. In his public statements, however, Reagan continued to assert that the Soviets were doomed. In one of his first speeches after being shot, in May 1981, Reagan told graduating students at Notre Dame, "The West won't contain communism, it will transcend it. . . . It will dismiss it as some bizarre chapter in human history, whose last pages are even now being written."

His initial hopes were focused on Poland, where the Solidarity labor movement was challenging the Soviet-backed regime. "Their economy is going bust," he wrote in his diary. "Here is the 1st major break in the Red dike—Poland's disenchantment with the Soviet Union." At a press conference in June, the first question was about Poland and Soviet domination of Eastern Europe. Reagan replied, "It's not a normal way of living for human beings. . . . I think we are seeing the beginning cracks, the beginning of the end." After the government of Poland declared martial law, Reagan got even more excited, writing, "We can't let this revolution against Communism fail without offering a hand. We may never have an opportunity like this one in our lifetime." Recognizing that his options were limited, however, he settled for covert assistance to Solidarity and a modest program of economic sanctions, forgoing those that would hurt American companies.

In the early years, Richard Pipes was the most influential of Reagan's hard-liners. A Jewish refugee who had escaped Poland in 1940, Pipes had become a leading Russia scholar at Harvard before joining the NSC as its top Soviet specialist. He saw the Russian character as inherently brutal and tyrannical, and shared Kirkpatrick's view of communism as incapable of evolution. Pipes briefed Reagan directly on the Soviets and wrote the directive delineating his policy of forcing change in the Communist world, National Security Decision Directive 75. This secret paper, which Reagan signed in January 1983, laid out an effort "to contain and over time reverse Soviet expansionism by competing effectively with the Soviet Union in all international arenas" and making clear to Moscow "that unacceptable behavior will incur costs that would outweigh any gains." Under the policy known as linkage, arms control negotiations and trade agreements were to be treated not as ends in themselves but as rewards for better behavior. The directive is more vague about punishments: "In the longer term, if Soviet behavior should worsen, e.g., an invasion of Poland, we would need to consider extreme measures."

Externally, Reagan's greatest support was British prime minister Margaret Thatcher. He had formed a friendship with her on a trip to Great Britain in 1975, when she was the Tory opposition leader. The bond was renewed when she visited him in Washington a month after his inauguration, and again during the summer of 1981. Thatcher's parallel attack on the more comprehensive British welfare state encouraged the idea that the world was experiencing a global antistatist tide. But Reagan took pains to distinguish democratic socialism in Western Europe from the Communist tyranny in the East, whose demise he proclaimed again in his 1982 address to the British Parliament.

> In an ironic sense Karl Marx was right. We are witnessing today a great revolutionary crisis, a crisis where the demands of the economic order are conflicting directly with those of the political order. But the crisis is happening not in the free, non-Marxist West, but in the home of Marxist-Leninism, the Soviet Union. It is the Soviet Union that runs against the tide of history by denying human freedom and human dignity to its citizens.

Reagan went on to discuss the "decay of the Soviet experiment" and to argue that "any system is inherently unstable that has no peaceful means to legitimize its leaders." In the final section, he played off a famous line of Trotsky's in elaborating his "plan and hope" that "the march of freedom and democracy . . . will leave Marxism-Leninism on the ash-heap of history as it has left other tyrannies which stifle the freedom and muzzle the self-expression of the people." Anthony Dolan, a protégé of William F. Buckley, drafted the speech, but much of this language was Reagan's.

Reagan's more famous expression of the same view came in his "Evil Empire" speech to the National Association of Evangelicals in Orlando in March 1983. Rallying Christian groups against the nuclear freeze proposal being debated in Congress, the president branded the Soviet Union "the focus of evil in the modern world." Reagan crossed out the words "now and forever" in Dolan's draft. He offered instead an assertion about its impermanence. "I believe that Communism is another sad, bizarre chapter in human history whose last pages are now being written."

The administration did not scruple about the methods it used in helping to write them. During the campaign, Reagan had promised to "unleash the CIA," which had refrained from covert operations in the aftermath of the 1975 Church Committee hearings and revelations about black bag jobs and assassination plots. The unleashing fell to Reagan's former campaign manager William Casey, an advocate of counterinsurgency operations who had worked for the Office of Strategic Services (OSS), the ancestor of the CIA during the Second World War. In one episode still shrouded in classification, the CIA developed a scheme to sabotage a trans-Siberian natural gas pipeline by feeding the Soviets computer software containing a Trojan horse virus. The result of this early episode of cyber warfare, as former secretary of the air force Thomas C. Reed revealed many years later, was a nuclear-size explosion in the Siberian wilderness in 1982.

But direct confrontation was the exception. Most of the stepped-up conflict would take place through proxies in the developing world. This idea came to be known as the Reagan Doctrine, a term coined by the columnist Charles Krauthammer to describe a policy of rollback as opposed to mere containment of the Soviet Union. Reagan thought the most urgent place to take a stand was Central America, where Nicaragua had fallen to the Communists and where, Secretary of State Haig alleged, the Soviets had a "hit list" of countries slated for takeover. Reagan saw this as an especially dangerous signal: one of his favorite fake Lenin quotes was "Once we have Latin America, we won't have to take the United States, the last bastion of capitalism, because it will fall into our outstretched hands like over-ripe fruit." He believed that President Kennedy had been wrong to abandon the Bay of Pigs invaders in 1961. The fact that Cuban advisers were helping the new Sandinista government in Nicaragua underscored his distress.

Reagan exaggerated the terribleness of the Nicaraguan regime and the virtues of the right-wing rebels, the Contras, whom he called "the moral equivalent of the founding fathers." In 1981, he authorized Casey to cut off the flow of Soviet arms to Central America. His larger goals were to undermine the Sandinistas and prop up the brutal military regime in neighboring El Salvador.

Many American liberals argued that Reagan's policy amounted to backing for death squads and massive violations of human rights. As the CIA trained the Contras, Democrats in Congress advocated a negotiated settlement in Nicaragua and tried to limit Reagan's freedom of action by passing the Boland Amendment (named for Edward P. Boland, the chairman of the House Intelligence Committee), which prohibited aiding the Contras in their attempt to overthrow the Nicaraguan government.

Other battlegrounds in the proxy conflict with the Soviets included Afghanistan and Angola. Reagan believed that President Carter's response to the Soviet invasion of Afghanistan in 1979, which included a grain embargo and a boycott of the 1980 Olympics, was far too weak. He authorized the CIA to supply the mujahideen fighters resisting the Soviet occupation with shoulder-fired Stinger missiles that could bring down planes and helicopters or force them to fly too high for effective action. Covert subversion in Afghanistan was soon costing three hundred million dollars a year. In Angola, where Cuban and Soviet advisers were supporting the Marxist government in a brutal postcolonial civil war, the CIA delivered weapons and other assistance to Jonas Savimbi's National Union for the Total Independence of Angola. Savimbi became a frequent guest at the Heritage Foundation and the White House. Additional funds went to Cambodians fighting the Communist government of Vietnam.

In Poland, Reagan coordinated a nonlethal policy of destabilizing the Communist regime with the Vatican. Pope John Paul II came from Poland and was perhaps the only other world leader who shared Reagan's intuitions about communism's vulnerability. His 1979 trip back to his home country, which featured millions of Poles chanting, "We want God! We want God!" helped ignite the Solidarity movement. Meeting the pope for the first time at the Vatican in June 1982, Reagan expressed his own view that religion might prove to be the Soviets' Achilles' heel. Like Reagan, John Paul II had survived an assassination attempt in 1981, and he and Reagan shared their belief that God had kept them alive for a special purpose. He had no power, however, to keep the jet-lagged president awake. Reagan fell asleep while the pope was talking, a moment captured on tape by NBC and shown on *Nightly News*.

Reagan's idiosyncratic view of the Soviet Union as weak and vulnerable pointed him in two contradictory directions. The more apparent one was confrontational. The less visible was conciliatory. He had a heartfelt horror of nuclear weapons and was sincere in saying he opposed the unratified SALT II Treaty because it didn't go far enough. When Caspar Weinberger tried to persuade him to ignore the treaty's limits on submarine-based missiles, Reagan sided with Secretary of State George Shultz (who had replaced Alexander Haig in 1982) and decreed that the United States would abide by the terms of SALT II, even though he knew the Soviets were violating them. He genuinely desired better relations to reduce the risk of Armageddon, a biblical prophecy he took seriously. An aerie of hawks obscured Reagan's dovish side. But it was there all along.

11

They Keep Dying on Me

Because of Afghanistan, relations with the Soviets were already bad when Reagan took office. In the first days of the administration, the Soviet leader Leonid Brezhnev wrote to the new president requesting a summit meeting—a goodwill gesture somewhat obscured by the boilerplate condemning of American militarism and imperialism. Reagan dismissed the overture, in keeping with Alexander Haig's admonition that arms control and trade benefits had to be conditioned on Soviet conduct, and in particular on restraining Fidel Castro. But then Reagan was shot, and he woke up possessed of the idea that God had saved him for the purpose of preventing nuclear war. Now he wanted to answer Brezhnev.

From his hospital bed, he wrote a conciliatory response asking for a "meaningful and constructive dialogue which will assist us in fulfilling our joint obligation to finding lasting peace." As a token of friendship, Reagan offered something he intended to do anyway for domestic political reasons: lift the grain embargo imposed by Carter in response to the Soviet invasion of Afghanistan. These messages were embedded in a heartfelt expression of his political philosophy. "The peoples of the world, despite differences in racial and ethnic origin, have very much in common," Reagan wrote. "They want the dignity of having some control over their individual destiny. They want to work at the craft or trade of their own choosing and to be fairly rewarded. They want to raise their families in peace without harming anyone or suffering harm themselves. Government exists for their convenience, not the other way around."

His draft greatly alarmed his foreign policy circle, who wondered what had happened to the president's distrust of the Soviets. Haig, committed to the policy of linkage, tried to talk him out of lifting the grain embargo and sending the letter, which he proposed replacing with a State Department version complaining about the Soviet military buildup. "I need to follow my own instincts. And I'm going to," Reagan told Deaver. In the end, Reagan sent both: the State Department indictment, along with a handwritten version of his personal overture as a cover letter. Whether because he found the letter provocative or because he was addled from his addiction to sleeping pills and by a series of small strokes, Brezhnev sent what Reagan described as an "icy reply."

Both sides were doing a fine job of misintepreting each other's signals. Hearing Reagan's charged rhetoric and his claims about Soviet nuclear superiority that they knew weren't true, Soviet officials began to believe that the United States was pursuing a first-strike capability, if not planning an actual first strike. In May 1981 the KGB advised its stations in the West that the United States might be preparing an attack and asked them to relay any additional warning signs. The equivalent misunderstanding on Reagan's part was that the Soviets viewed nuclear war as winnable and were trying to gain an edge, while still pursuing a strategy of world revolution.

As a result of these mutual misreadings, there would be no presidential summit meetings during Reagan's first term. This was partly a matter of successive Soviet leadership transitions, from Leonid Brezhnev to Yuri Andropov to Konstantin Chernenko to Mikhail Gorbachev in twenty-eight months. "They keep dying on me," Reagan joked. It was also a reflection of the Haig-Pipes view of Soviet proclivities and the confrontational policies outlined in NSDD 75. At the same time, Reagan kept looking for a way to open arms control talks that few others in his administration wanted. He read parts of his hospital letter to Brezhnev in a November 18 televised speech, his first major address on foreign policy. In it,

Reagan embraced the so-called zero option for intermediate-range missiles in Europe. America's NATO allies believed that Soviet SS-20 missiles deployed in Warsaw Pact countries in the 1970s had upset the balance of power. Their plan was to deploy new Cruise and Pershing II missiles to redress it, but the Soviets saw the more accurate American missiles as tilting the balance in the other direction. Reagan's offer was that the United States would cancel deployment of the Cruise and Pershing missiles if the Soviets removed their SS-20 missiles aimed at Western Europe.

Given that the zero option asked something for nothing—the Soviets' existing intermediate-range arsenal in exchange for the U.S. government agreeing not to deploy new missiles—it was unlikely to go anywhere. Nor did the plan take into account the independent nuclear arsenals of Britain and France. But while the sure-to-be-rejected proposal reflected a degree of cynicism on the part of advisers who didn't believe in arms control, Reagan was sincere in his desire for disarmament in broad strokes. His aides became adept at ignoring this side of his belief system, because they viewed it as impractical and contradictory to his calls for a military buildup. It surfaced again as he prepared for his first European trip in the summer of 1982, when Reagan announced that he was scrapping the framework of SALT, the Strategic Arms Limitation Treaty, in favor of START, the Strategic Arms Reduction Treaty. The world already had thirty thousand nuclear weapons, he said. Instead of merely curtailing the rate of increase, he wanted to reduce their absolute number.

With his military buildup funded, Reagan shelved his concern about a window of vulnerability. Even though the balance of power had shifted only in theory, he no longer felt that the United States was too weak to negotiate with the Soviets. Reagan's grasp of the particulars of nuclear strategy was always vague. Advisers noticed that he didn't appear to appreciate the differences among ground-based ballistic missiles, submarine-based missiles, and those dropped or fired from planes. He hadn't understood, for instance, that the Soviets possessed mostly land-based missiles. To Reagan, a nuke was a nuke. That meant that when he asked his aides for a bold offer to send to ongoing midlevel arms talks in Geneva, he was at their mercy. The proposal that resulted expressed his paradoxical demands, and quickly fell by the wayside. But Reagan's larger approach was coherent. He saw his military buildup as the path to successful negotiations, not an alternative to them. Despite the Orwellian ring of his slogan "Peace Through Strength," there was never any contradiction in Reagan's mind, and there turned out not to be much contradiction in practice. Reagan thought military superiority was the prerequisite for disarmament, and he wanted the latter to follow close on the heels of the former.

Most people took Reagan's stance as simple opposition to arms control, which gave rise to an enormous antinuclear movement in the West. Hundreds of thousands of people took to the streets in London and other European cities in 1981 to protest the American buildup. With the talks in Geneva stalled, the president now faced a risk that European allies might reject the U.S. missiles scheduled for deployment, fracturing NATO in the process. By 1982, there were large demonstrations in the United States supporting a nuclear freeze, culminating in a gathering of seven hundred thousand people in New York's Central Park in June 1982. That fall, the movement gathered momentum as Senators Ted Kennedy and Mark Hatfield announced their intention to introduce a freeze resolution in Congress.

Reagan saw the demand for unilateral disarmament as a parallel to appeasement before the Second World War. To him the idea was "a very dangerous fraud" that was rapidly gaining traction. In August 1982 the freeze resolution made it to the floor of the House, where it failed by only one vote. The issue deepened rifts in his own family, when his daughter Patti disavowed his policies at rallies and "No Nukes" concerts. The freeze movement's misconstrual of Reagan as a warmonger engendered a reciprocal misjudgment by Reagan himself, who thought he was in familiar territory. Applying a framework from the 1950s, he insisted that the Soviets had instigated the freeze movement, citing a Communist-dominated group called the World Peace Council. At the same time, he needed something to offer as an alternative.

The Strategic Defense Initiative (SDI) emerged out of the pressure from the freeze movement, Reagan's abhorrence of nuclear weapons, and an impasse over nuclear strategy; with congressional politics blocking the MX missile, hawks believed that America's ICBMs remained vulnerable. At a scientific level, the father of the idea was the nuclear physicist Edward Teller, the founder of the Lawrence Livermore National Laboratory. When Teller pitched space-based defense using X-ray lasers to the president in September 1982, Reagan embraced the idea as eminently logical. "Look, every weapon has resulted in a defense—the sword, then the shield," he said. At a political level, SDI owed its arrival to Robert "Bud" McFarlane, Reagan's deputy national security adviser. Despairing of a way to close the "window of vulnerability" without a viable plan for deploying the MX, McFarlane fastened on to the idea of space-based missile defense, which he'd heard about via Teller and others.

A savvy bureaucratic operator, McFarlane knew how to tee up the proposal. At a meeting with the Joint Chiefs of Staff on February 11, 1983, he arranged for military leaders to report promising progress on recent research. "Wouldn't it be better to protect the American people rather than avenge them?" General John Vessey, the chairman of the Joint Chiefs, asked the president. Then McFarlane weighed in: "For the first time in history what we are hearing here is that there may be another way which would enable you to defeat an attack by defending against it and over time relying less on nuclear weapons." As expected, Reagan latched on. "I understand," he said. "That's just what I've been hoping."

What McFarlane didn't anticipate was how swiftly and completely Reagan would become consumed by the concept. McFarlane saw missile defense mostly as a bluff. If made to sound sufficiently impressive, the research effort could be traded away for reductions in Soviet ICBMs—"the greatest sting operation in history," as he later put it. Reagan did not see the Strategic Defense Initiative as a bargaining chip or a sting operation. He saw it as an umbrella. His excitement is palpable in the diary entry he wrote after the Joint Chiefs' presentation, which echoed Vessey's words: "What if we were to tell the world that we want to protect our people not avenge them; that we are going to embark on a program of research to come up with a defensive weapon that could make nuclear weapons obsolete?"

Strategically, missile defense solved the problem of protecting American ICBMs from a first strike. Politically, it gave Reagan an answer to the freeze movement. Morally, it offered a way out of mutually assured destruction, offering him a new nuclear policy that wouldn't necessitate "dealing with other nations and human beings by threatening their existence." Psychologically, it was a great simplifying solution, a way to slice through what he experienced as the horrific muddle of nuclear strategy. Reagan couldn't wait to surprise the country with the good news. McFarlane and others thought his insistence on a March 23 announcement was wildly premature. Top defense officials saw the text of the president's speech only the night before. NATO allies and key congressional leaders had no notice at all. "Let me share with you a vision of the future which offers hope," Reagan told the nation that evening. "It is that we embark on a program to counter the awesome Soviet missile threat with measures that are defensive." The peroration appears in a draft in his own handwriting: "I call upon the scientific community in this country, who gave us nuclear weapons, to turn their great talents to the cause of mankind and world peace; to give us the means of rendering these weapons impotent and obsolete."

Coming just two weeks after his "evil empire" remarks, what immediately became known as the "Star Wars" speech threw the Soviet leadership into a panic. The new Soviet leader, Yuri Andropov, took it as confirmation that the United States had been planning an all-out nuclear attack and was now preparing to protect itself from retaliation. To the Soviets, Reagan's announcement heralded an arms race in space that they could ill afford and in which they lacked the technological expertise to compete. And wouldn't one side's ability to defend itself upset the balance of terror? Reagan understood that missile defense risked undermining deterrence. A week later, he came up with the solution: if the technology could be developed, he would share it with the enemy. Where the Soviets found his initial proposal terrifying, they considered the addendum preposterous.

• • •

Inside the White House, Reagan was more typically reactive, responding to what was brought to him. He asked few questions of his staff and seldom challenged them. He shunned conflict, responding with a joke or story to defuse tension and change the subject. This passivity lent itself to massive bureaucratic infighting. Reagan had appointed Haig as secretary of state on the basis of a personal recommendation from Richard Nixon. But power exacerbated Haig's paranoid and aggressive tendencies. After much nagging, he secured a promise that he would have full control of foreign policy. He then announced to the press that Reagan had made him the "vicar" of international affairs. "He didn't even want me as the president to be involved in setting foreign policy—he regarded it as his turf," Reagan noted in his memoirs. By mid-1982, Deaver was telling Reagan that Haig was a "cancer that has to be cut out." When Haig threatened resignation for the umpteenth time amid a crisis over the Israeli invasion of Lebanon, the troika persuaded Reagan finally to call his bluff.

Reagan's first national security adviser, Richard Allen, was out, too, resigning over a scandal involving a thousand dollars cash in an envelope from Japanese journalists interviewing Nancy Reagan, though no wrongdoing was ever proven. The replacements cut against each other. For State, Reagan chose George Shultz, a gravelly voiced former secretary of labor and secretary of the treasury in the Nixon administration with a background in academia and business. Shultz was a political moderate with an unreadable, self-contained style. But he could be petulant and, like Haig, often threatened to resign when he felt his integrity or his prerogatives were being challenged. To replace Allen, Reagan promoted his old friend William Clark. A lanky rancher in a Stetson hat and cowboy boots who kept a Colt .45 pistol on display in his office, "the Judge" was a more apt version of the John Wayne stereotype Europeans often applied to the president. Shultz, who did not share the hostility of the hawks to arms control agreements—or the neoconservative view that the Soviets would never change—arrived with the goal of improving relations between the superpowers. Clark came to prevent Deaver and Nancy Reagan from causing "an outbreak of world peace." Almost immediately, the two began a cat-and-mouse game, in which Clark blocked Shultz's access to Reagan and Shultz sought ways around him.

With Shultz's ascendancy, Reagan's peacemaking instincts began to round out his hawkish commitments. The new secretary of state elaborated a more conciliatory policy in a memo entitled "U.S.-Soviet Relations in 1983," sent two days after NSDD 75 and, implicitly, an answer to it. Though he was too wise to use the term, Shultz was essentially arguing for a resumption of détente—"intensified dialogue with Moscow." Finding Reagan eager for direct contact with Soviet officials, Shultz circumvented Clark, getting Deaver to help him sneak Anatoly Dobrynin, the longtime Soviet ambassador, into the White House for a secret meeting with the president. Reagan asked Dobrynin for the release of seven Christian Pentecostalists who had sought asylum in the U.S. embassy in Moscow and were living in the basement. He also proposed a back door for direct communication with the Kremlin via Shultz. "If you are ready to move forward, so are we," he told Dobrynin.

From that point on, Reagan generally preferred Shultz's conciliatory views to the confrontation of Clark and Pipes. "Some of the N.S.C. staff are too hard line & don't think any approach should be made to the Soviets," he wrote in his diary in April 1983. "I think I'm hard-line & will never appease but I do want to try & let them see there is a better world if they'll show by deed they want to get along with the free world." When Pipes left the NSC to return to Harvard, Reagan passed over Pipes's uncompromising disciple John Lenczowski in favor of Jack Matlock, a career foreign service officer allied with Shultz.

In July 1983, Reagan drafted another personal letter, this one to Yuri Andropov, the former head of the KGB, who had succeeded Brezhnev. "If we can agree on mutual, verifiable reductions in the number of nuclear weapons we both hold, could this not be a first step toward the elimination of all such weapons? What a blessing this would be for the people we both represent," he wrote. "You and I have the ability to bring this about through our negotiators in the arms reduction talks." Reagan gave the draft to Clark, who believed that it made the United States look too eager for arms control, and urged Reagan to take out all references to eliminating nuclear weapons. Reagan reluctantly acceded, redrafting the letter as an anodyne request for dialogue, though he emphasized again his wish for a way to circumvent the bureaucracy in communicating. Officials noted Andropov's shaky handwriting in his response. They thought he might be suffering from stress. The kidney disease that would kill him a few months later was a well-kept secret.

Clark's star was in rapid descent. He overplayed his hand when he sent Reagan a memo arguing that Shultz was a "solid economist" who had no business meddling in Soviet policy. Shultz caught wind of the memo and threatened to resign. Reagan begged him to stay, offering him enhanced authority. Crucially, Nancy Reagan—upset about a *Time* cover that called Clark "the second most important man in the White House"—sided with Shultz, and began lobbying her husband to replace his national security adviser again.

Shultz's efforts to thaw superpower relations stalled abruptly on September 1, 1983, when a Soviet fighter plane shot down a Korean Air Lines passenger jet that had strayed into Soviet airspace, killing all 269 people aboard, including Congressman Larry McDonald, who happened to be the president of the John Birch Society, and sixty other American citizens. The Soviets made matters worse by issuing a preposterous denial that they had shot down the plane, and then insisting that the plane was on a spying mission. It wasn't, of course, although American fighter jets had increased the risk of a hair-trigger response by aggressively challenging the Soviet Union's air perimeter over the preceding months.

Reagan resisted calls for significant punitive action, but further inflamed the issue with his language in a televised speech from the Oval Office a few days later, where he called the shootdown a "massacre," "savagery," and a "crime against humanity." He also advanced a claim others in his administration rejected, that the Soviets had downed the civilian airliner on purpose. The Soviets responded with archaic propaganda describing Reagan as a madman and comparing him to Hitler. In a statement issued from his secret VIP hospital, Andropov said that any improvement in U.S.-Soviet relations would be essentially impossible so long as Reagan remained in office.

The next international shocks came in rapid succession. On October 23 a truck bomb killed 241 U.S. Marines in their barracks in Beirut, where they were deployed as part of a multinational peacekeeping mission following Israel's withdrawal of its occupying force. Two days later, Reagan approved an invasion of Grenada, a tiny Caribbean island of 110,000 people. Maurice Bishop, the country's late ruler, was a Cuban-backed Black Power revolutionary who had been assassinated by members of his own movement who deemed him insufficiently radical and, in Reagan's view, because he wanted better relations with the United States.

Reagan's televised address about these two events, which he rewrote heavily himself, displayed both his limitations as a thinker and his tremendous gifts as a communicator. The military had gone into Grenada to rescue nearly a thousand American medical students placed in jeopardy by a violent coup. But Reagan framed both interventions as responses to Soviet aggression. "The events in Lebanon and Grenada, though oceans apart, are closely related," he said. "Not only has Moscow assisted and encouraged the violence in both countries, but it provides direct support through a network of surrogates and terrorists. It is no coincidence that when the thugs tried to wrest control over Grenada, there were 30 Soviet advisers and hundreds of Cuban military and paramilitary forces on the island."

In reality, the events were not related to each other, and only Grenada had anything to do with the Cold War. Hezbollah and Iran were the likely culprits in the Lebanon bombing, though they didn't take credit for it. The real significance of the Grenada invasion was as an expression of resurgent U.S. nationalism, and in the confident and effective use of the U.S. military. Reagan had tears in his eyes as he watched American students "lean down and kiss American soil the moment they stepped off the airplanes that brought them home." This was the old lifeguard on duty, rescuing people he didn't know, who would probably never thank him.

The Soviets misread Grenada as a sign of greater aggression to come. Soon after the tiny war, the United States and NATO were scheduled to conduct a military exercise called Able Archer, designed to test their nuclear command-and-control processes. Able Archer was an annual event, but this particular version of the exercise was more elaborate, involving the defense ministers of several NATO countries as well as the president and vice president themselves. A theory at the KGB held that if the United States were going to launch a nuclear strike, it would use a military exercise as cover. Now, against the backdrop of heightened tensions— Star Wars, the "Evil Empire" speech, the Korean airliner, and Grenada—KGB officials read the electronic signals as evidence that the United States was preparing a surprise attack on the Soviet Union.

Though the Able Archer exercise ended without incident, this was probably the most dangerous moment in the Cold War since the Cuban Missile Crisis. That same month, Soviet negotiators walked out of both the START talks in Geneva and conventional force limitation talks in Vienna. At the end of 1983, for the first time in many years, there were no active discussions between the superpowers. When Reagan learned about the Soviet misinterpretation of Able Archer, by way of a KGB double agent working for the British, he expressed shock that the Soviets could see the United States as a potential nuclear aggressor. It made him, he wrote in his diary, "even more anxious to get a top Soviet leader in a room alone and try to convince him that we had no designs on the Soviet Union and the Russians had nothing to fear from us."

Lowering tensions was a political imperative for him as well. With the 1984 election less than a year away, Reagan faced a problem. His pollster Richard Wirthlin reported that a majority of the public disapproved of his foreign policy, with a significant percentage saying that his handling of Soviet relations was increasing the risk of war. Inside the White House, the troika put the blame on Clark for undermining disarmament discussions. The opportunity for Reagan to replace him arrived when Secretary of the Interior James Watt was forced to resign over the bigoted comments he made while attempting to lampoon affirmative action. Reagan shifted Clark to the Interior Department, where he could only be an improvement, and promoted McFarlane to national security adviser.

Clark's departure made all the difference. McFarlane didn't try to keep Shultz away from the president. The secretary of state now had a clear path to reopen the START talks. Reagan was ready to make a deal as well, believing that he could now negotiate from a position of strength. The president sent Andropov another conciliatory personal message on Christmas Eve 1983. But having just walked out of talks, the Soviets weren't ready to return.

Reagan spoke to the American public in January 1984, acknowledging that relations with the Soviets were bad and vowing to engage in dialogue. "My dream is to see the day when nuclear weapons will be banished from the face of the earth," he said. The most heartfelt passage in his televised address was a parable of his own devising about a Russian couple named Ivan and Anya meeting an American couple named Jim and Sally. Supposing away the language barrier, the two couples wouldn't debate their differences— they would become friends. He concluded with a plea to the Soviet leadership to do the same. "Let us begin now," he said. The press missed the significance of this slightly goofy allegory, just as it had overlooked Reagan naming Shultz as the administration's chief spokesman on arms control and other peacemaking gestures.

The Soviets themselves, thoroughly persuaded of Reagan's hostility, dismissed his warmer tone as an election-year ploy. They had worries of their own: Andropov died in February 1984 and was succeeded by Konstantin Chernenko. Reagan once again found reason to believe that this leader would be different. "I have a gut feeling I'd like to talk to him about our problems man to man & see if I could convince him there would be a material benefit to the Soviets if they'd join the family of nations etc.," he confided to his diary. The president sent another handwritten note, assuring the new Soviet premier that the United States had no offensive intentions. On the rush translation of Chernenko's droning response,

Reagan noted, "I think this calls for a very well thought out reply & not a routine acknowledgement that leaves the status quo as is." He appended another handwritten note to his response, telling Chernenko, "I want you to know that neither I nor the American people hold any offensive intentions toward you or the Soviet people."

These are poignant communications: a president seeking a pen pal, reaching out in the most personal way he could to a series of ghosts. Gasping with emphysema, Chernenko failed to appreciate Reagan's overtures. The Kremlin hard-liners saw arms control negotiations the same way the American hard-liners did: as a carrot to reward improved behavior by the enemy. The Soviets refused to meet unless the United States withdrew its new missiles from Europe. Only then would the Soviets discuss what *they* wanted to talk about: banning weapons in space. In May 1984 they announced they were pulling out of the upcoming Olympics in Los Angeles, reciprocity for the U.S. boycott in 1980. Reagan didn't help matters that summer when he performed a microphone check before recording his regular Saturday radio address. "My fellow Americans," he ad-libbed, "I am pleased to tell you today that I've signed legislation that will outlaw Russia forever. We begin bombing in five minutes."

Reagan and Shultz weren't to be deflected from their new course, however. When Shultz told Reagan that the Soviet foreign minister, Andrei Gromyko, was interested in coming to Washington to meet with him, Reagan seized at the opening, despite Gromyko's reputation for humorless rigidity. Meeting with Gromyko in the Oval Office, the president asked him to stay afterward for a private word. Then he said something that wasn't in his official talking points. He wanted to eliminate nuclear weapons completely.

12

Morning Again in America

Both the president's wife and his best friend in the administration opposed his running for reelection. Nancy was afraid he would be assassinated and was eager to return to California. Bill Clark thought he was slipping mentally. Many others made similar observations. Reagan's fog had grown thicker since the assassination attempt. His hearing was worse, his memory was hazier, and he tired more easily. He repeated himself in a way that made people crazy.

There is no indication, however, that Reagan seriously contemplated not running for reelection. By late 1983 the combination of tax cuts and deficit spending was delivering a tremendous Keynesian boost to the economy. GDP rose 4.6 percent that year. It would rise 7.3 percent in 1984, the economy's best annual performance in two decades. The stimulus goosed job creation, and with it Reagan's approval rating, which after the Grenada invasion crossed the 50 percent threshold for the first time since 1981. According to his pollster Richard Wirthlin, Reagan's only significant liability was the fear that he was trigger-happy and more likely than a Democrat to get the country into a war.

Ten fifty-five p.m. on a Sunday night was an odd time for Reagan to announce he was running again, but no one took this as a clue that his wife was consulting an oracle. "When I first addressed you from here, our national defenses were dangerously weak, we had suffered humiliation in Iran, and at home we were adrift, possibly because of a failure here in Washington to trust the courage and character of you, the people," Reagan told the nation on January 28, 1984. "But worst of all, we were on the brink of economic collapse from years of government overindulgence and abusive over-taxation." Three years later, he said, the economy was humming, God had returned to the public schools, and America was "back and standing tall." Reagan's rhetorical turn was to give credit, not take it. "You were magnificent as we pulled the Nation through the long night of our national calamity," he declared.

That announcement established the tone for Reagan's positive and patriotic reelection campaign, which showed the country a flattering, congratulatory portrait of itself. Its epitome was a television commercial built around the declaration "It's morning again in America." Against a backdrop of people going to work, getting married, and raising the flag, the voice-over noted reductions in unemployment, inflation, and mortgage rates. "Under the leadership of President Reagan, our country is prouder and stronger and better," it asserted. "Why would we ever want to return to where we were less than four short years ago?" Campaign stops featured the president regaling heartland audiences with his genial humor in picturesque settings. The cheering crowds responded with the chant "USA! USA! USA!"

In contrast to 1980, Reagan did not come bearing an agenda for change. While he continued to inveigh against the federal government, he didn't specify how he might take another swing at it. Because he faced no primary challenge, Reagan was able to position himself toward the center from the beginning of the election. Despite vocal agitation for banning abortion at the Republican convention in Dallas, he steered clear of his more frantic allies on the religious right, invoking again the transcendent vision of America as "a shining city on a hill." The Democratic convention in San Francisco, by contrast, pulled the party's nominee, former vice president Walter Mondale, closer to its constituent groups: government workers, public school teachers, African Americans, feminists, and labor unions. After winning the nomination, Mondale chose as his chief lines of attack Reagan's failure to engage in talks with the Soviets and the two-hundred-billion-dollar budget deficit. Reagan barely engaged with either issue, brushing off criticism and taking a relentlessly upbeat approach.

Reagan's age showed in the first of two presidential debates, when he referred to military uniforms as "wardrobe," spoke haltingly, and seemed to lose his train of thought while answering a question about taxes. "My heart sank as he floundered his way through his responses, fumbling with his notes, uncharacteristically lost for words. He looked tired and bewildered," his son Ron Jr. later wrote, speculating that his father was already exhibiting signs of Alzheimer's. But Reagan rallied in the second debate, which focused on international affairs. When asked whether as the oldest president to serve he had the vigor for another term, he deadpanned his response, "I will not make age an issue of this campaign. I am not going to exploit, for political purposes, my opponent's youth and inexperience." Mondale joined in the laughter, but knew. "That was really the end of my campaign that night," he said later.

Reagan won forty-nine states and 59 percent of the popular vote. The results indicated a continued shift of traditionally Democratic voters to the Republican column. After the election, the Democratic pollster Stanley Greenberg examined voting patterns in Macomb County, Michigan, an area just outside Detroit. The white, ethnic voters who lived there had voted 63 percent for John F. Kennedy in 1960 and 75 percent for Lyndon Johnson in 1964. In 1984, 66 percent of them voted for Ronald Reagan. Greenberg contended that the white working class no longer identified with a Democratic Party that it saw shifting resources to African Americans. What this analysis tended to ignore was the valid aspects of Reagan's critique of social programs. Twenty years on, the Great Society was in many respects sustaining a culture of poverty. Mondale suffered for failing to acknowledge any failures of past liberal policy or any successes of Reaganomics.

In his second inaugural address, Reagan framed his version of American exceptionalism in grand terms: "restoring the promise that is offered to every citizen in this, the last best hope of man on earth." Reagan referred to "this breed called Americans" as "special among the nations of the earth." He promised to "do whatever needs to be done to preserve this last and greatest bastion of freedom." The idea that American confidence was back after the funk of the late 1970s was echoed in economic statistics and in the national mood; in 1979, 84 percent of the public told Gallup they were dissatisfied with the way things were going in America. By 1986 only 26 percent felt that way.

As Reagan's second term began, the presentation of the presidency had never before been so well managed. Michael Deaver turned the White House into a national soundstage, lavishing attention on backdrops, lighting, and camera angles. The president's theatrical training was a huge asset in the creation of media moments. Reagan followed stage markings precisely and took direction like a pro. He would show up on time and well prepared, stand in the right place, and smile on cue. He always dressed properly for the occasion, whether it was clearing brush at his ranch or working at his desk.

His public performance reflected not celebrity values, but the ethic of a pre-1960s Hollywood. At state dinners, the Reagans favored a style of entertainment that was accessible, uplifting, and—to younger people—a bit dated. Neil Diamond sang at a dinner for Prince Charles and Princess Diana; Julio Iglesias for François Mitterrand; and Frank Sinatra for the president of Sri Lanka. Nancy Reagan hosted *In Performance at the White House*, a series on PBS, featuring Liza Minnelli, Bobby Short, and Marvin Hamlisch.

One of the more astonishing relics from this era was the *All-Star Tribute to Ronald "Dutch" Reagan* that CBS broadcast in late 1985. The program embodies the feeling of media capitulation to Reagan that took hold after his second landslide. The president's popularity and affability made the notion of one of the Big Three networks staging a black-tie homage to him strangely uncontroversial. Filmed on a soundstage designed as a cabaret, the program blended the cultures of old Hollywood and new Washington. It was organized by Variety Clubs International, a charity supporting medical care for poor children, which marked the occasion by dedicating a Ronald Reagan Wing at a hospital in Omaha, Nebraska.

One might have asked why poor children should be required to seek charity for life-saving medical care, but no one did. Instead, Reagan's Hollywood friends sang, danced, and told jokes. Frank Sinatra, the host, began by singing "Have Yourself a Merry Little Christmas." The comedian Dean Martin sang "Mr. Wonderful," pretending to be drunk—or perhaps actually drunk. Ben Vereen and the child performer Emmanuel Lewis tap-danced and sang "Hooray for Hollywood." Steve Lawrence and Eydie Gormé, the duo of lounge singers popular in the 1950s, performed a song written for the occasion, "America Is Changing Back to What She Used to Be": "A feeling's moving through her that is wild and fresh and free / So let's celebrate her spirit and her rediscovered pride / Let's sing the song that burns deep down inside."

Theories of Reagan's success were the currency in Washington after his reelection. Was he acting his way through the presidency? Was he blessed with incredible luck? Congresswoman Pat Schroeder of Colorado astutely observed that his was a "Teflon presidency: nothing stuck." When Reagan blundered by agreeing to a request from the German chancellor Helmut Kohl to lay a wreath at the military cemetery in Bitburg to commemorate the fortieth anniversary of the surrender of the Nazis, the Washington firestorm that ensued was fierce but brief. Few believed Reagan had any malice in him, so when he stumbled he was quickly excused. His increasing haziness ensured that when something went wrong, those around him were held responsible.

In the first half of his second term, Reagan was also benefiting from Peggy Noonan's speechwriting, the best he'd ever had. Noonan, like Reagan, came from radio, and had a way with the spoken word. She shared his narrative and sentimental frame of mind, his faith in America's fundamental goodness. In memorial speeches such as "The Boys of Pointe du Hoc," which Reagan delivered to a circle of veterans on a Normandy beachhead on the fortieth anniversary of D-day in 1984, she caught better than anyone else what the political scientist Hugh Heclo calls Reagan's "sacramental vision," his misty framing of American patriotism as civic religion. When the space shuttle *Challenger* blew up shortly after its launch in January 1986, Noonan borrowed from a poet who served in the Royal Canadian Air Force in World War II to depict the seven dead astronauts as brave pioneers who had "slipped the surly bonds of earth to touch the face of God."

Henry Kissinger once said that Reagan wasn't interested in policy and only cared about the question of what to say publicly. Speeches were indeed the most important component of Reagan's leadership style, the way he persuaded people, put pressure on Congress, and assured his conservative allies that his compromises didn't affect his fundamental commitments. Public speaking was also the way he brought others serving in his administration into alignment with his beliefs. Reagan's ability with language was considerable. The handwritten edits on his speech drafts testify to his skill at transforming bureaucratic language into vivid, human conversation.

Eloquence, entertainment, and stagecraft filled the programmatic vacuum left by Reagan's content-free reelection campaign. He ignored pressure from the right to pursue an agenda centered on abortion and other social issues, just as he tuned out pressure from liberals to talk about AIDS. In practice, his policy options had become much more limited. The deficit, which remained at 5 percent of GDP in 1985 and 1986, foreclosed the possibility of further tax cuts. Other than miscellaneous proposals for housing vouchers and block grants, his challenge to the welfare state had played itself out.

Reagan's most powerful impact on social policy came indirectly, through the judges he appointed. Inside the White House, Edwin Meese developed procedures to ensure more consistently conservative nominees to the federal bench. Many of the names the president's legal advisers brought forward were connected to the Federalist Society, the influential conservative legal organization Meese had helped found. Antonin Scalia, whom Reagan named to the Supreme Court in 1986, was the most forceful exponent of the Federalist Society's belief in interpreting the Constitution according to its literal meaning and original intent. By the time Scalia's nomination sailed through the Senate, scores of Reagan's lower-level judicial appointees were already at work reversing decades of

liberal drift in areas ranging from economic regulation to affirmative action and the rights of the accused. Reagan's 376 federal court
appointments remain the highest total of any president. This
includes his three Supreme Court appointees (four if one counts the
promotion of William H. Rehnquist to chief justice), eighty-
three U.S. Court of Appeals judges, and 290 district court judges.

The legislative accomplishments of Reagan's second term were
the pet ideas of senators which Reagan adopted as his own: Bill Brad-
ley's tax reform, Alan Simpson's immigration reform, and Daniel
Patrick Moynihan's welfare reform. Of these, the concept of radically
simplifying the tax code by lowering rates and eliminating loop-
holes and deductions was the most significant. The highest federal
tax rates in 1985 were 50 percent for individuals and 46 percent for
corporations. The legislation Reagan signed in 1986 collapsed fourteen brackets to three while setting the top rates at 28 and 34 percent.
Capital gains and dividends were taxed as ordinary income, promoting economic efficiency. Tax reform was also Reagan's most
important intervention on behalf of the working poor, taking some
six million people off the rolls completely and expanding the Earned
Income Tax Credit, an explicitly redistributive program designed to
lift low-paid workers above the poverty line.

On immigration, Reagan's instincts were rooted in his experience
living in Southern California, where the movement of unskilled
workers across the border served the interests of farmers, consum-
ers, and migrants themselves. "I believe in the idea of amnesty for
those who have put down roots and lived here, even though some-
time back they may have entered illegally," he said in his 1984 debate
with Mondale. In November 1986, Reagan signed the Simpson-
Mazzoli Act, which gave legal status to three million undocumented
residents and allowed seasonal movement across the border by farm
laborers. The bill also aimed to eliminate the incentive to immigrate
illegally by making it a crime for employers knowingly to hire undocumented workers. "The legalization provisions in this act will go far
to improve the lives of a class of individuals who must not hide in the
shadows, without access to many of the benefits of a free and open
society," Reagan wrote in a signing statement.

But without an agenda, Reagan drifted from his principles of free markets, deregulation, and individual self-sufficiency. When the falling value of the Japanese yen put America's Big Three automakers in peril, he intervened to protect the industry by imposing import quotas on Japanese cars. As in California, he became increasingly supportive of environmental regulation, expanding wildlife refuges and extending the Clean Water Act. After the Democrats reclaimed a Senate majority with a gain of eight seats in the 1986 midterm election, the administration's domestic policy became even more reactive. Reagan embraced liberal social policy in 1988 when he signed the Family Support Act, sponsored by Senator Moynihan, on the theory that it promoted work and personal responsibility. In fact, the law significantly increased welfare spending in exchange for adding modest incentives for beneficiaries to work.

The lack of more ambitious domestic goals is partly attributable to staff changes in the second term, which caused the functioning of the administration to grow bumpier. All three members of the troika left the White House staff in 1985: Meese to become attorney general, Baker to become secretary of the treasury, and Deaver to become a lobbyist. Donald Regan, who swapped jobs with Baker, was now chief of staff. An imperious man lacking deep ties to the president, he swiftly incurred the dislike of the second most important person in the White House, the president's wife.

13

Why Wait Until the Year 2000?

After his reelection, Reagan sat for an interview with *Time*. "I just happen to believe that we cannot go into another generation with the world living under the threat of those weapons and knowing that some madman can push the button some place . . . ," he said. "My hope has been, and my dream, that we can get the Soviet Union to join us in starting verifiable reductions of the weapons. Once you start down that road, they've got to see how much better off we would both be if we got rid of them entirely." In his dealing with the Soviets, Reagan's two terms were almost those of two different presidents. Both the hard-liner and the peacemaker were present throughout, but the balance shifted so decisively from one to the other as to create a discontinuity. The man who had denounced the nuclear freeze as Soviet propaganda was now suggesting not just reduction but elimination of all nuclear weapons. In some ways this evolution echoed his move from left to right while working for GE during the 1950s.

What explains Reagan's remarkable transformation from Cold War hawk to nuclear peacemaker? His nuclear abolitionism had deep roots, going back to flirtation with pacifism in the early 1930s. His antiwar side was connected to narratives and images that deeply affected him: seeing *Journey's End* with the Cleavers in Rockford in 1929, being shown footage from the liberation of Auschwitz at Fort Roach in 1945, and watching the ABC television movie *The Day After* in 1983. A projection that stuck with him was that at least 150 million Americans—two-thirds of the population in 1980—would be killed in an all-out nuclear war, though he believed for some reason that Soviet losses would be limited to a much smaller percentage. He was appalled by advisers who "tossed around macabre jargon about 'throw weights' and 'kill ratios' as if they were talking about baseball scores." In his diary and to aides, Reagan worried that the biblical prophecy of Armageddon was at hand.

With the elevation of Mikhail Gorbachev as the new Soviet leader in March 1985, Reagan's hopes for a nuclear peace rose again. Ever since his hospital letter to Brezhnev, the president had been looking for a counterpart on whom he could unleash his persuasive powers. He was desperate enough to convince himself that the wheezing apparatchiks Andropov and Chernenko might be reformers. When Chernenko died from emphysema, Reagan sent Vice President Bush to the funeral with a letter inviting Gorbachev to a summit meeting in the United States. He needed to explain to him that the United States meant no harm.

Reagan had two crucial supports in his shift to peacemaking, one familiar and the other hidden. The familiar one was Secretary of State George Shultz, who shared both Reagan's eccentric belief in the vulnerability of the Soviet system and his dream of nuclear disarmament. Shultz was less fervent about the former, but had a better idea how to go about achieving the latter. It was Shultz who let Reagan be Reagan in his dealings with the Soviets, in large part by beating back the hard-liners in the administration. Over the strenuous objections and devious leaks of Weinberger and Casey, Shultz revived the Geneva disarmament talks in January 1985 by agreeing to put SDI on the table as a topic for discussion. Shultz counseled Reagan that the new Soviet leader represented meaningful change, challenging Casey's view that Gorbachev was more of the same. "Gorbachev's letter is also notable for its non-polemical tone," Shultz wrote in a memo to Reagan analyzing Gorbachev's response to his invitation to Washington. "In fact, his message seems to be that we should both tone down public rhetoric and do business in a calm way that avoids 'deepening our differences' and 'whipping up animosity.'"

Reagan knew how dependent his ambitions were on Shultz. Whenever his secretary of state threatened to resign in a fit of pique or out of exhaustion, Reagan talked him off the ledge. When internal disputes flared, he usually took Shultz's side. "Cap and Bill have views contrary to George's on S. Am., the middle East & our arms negotiations," Reagan wrote in his diary after his reelection. "It's so out of hand George sounds like he wants out. I can't let this happen. Actually George is carrying out my policy. I'm going to meet with Cap & Bill and lay it out to them. Wont be fun but it has to be done." Conflict averse as always, Reagan never did get around to laying it out for Weinberger and Casey, which kept Shultz battling with them, but mostly prevailing.

The second figure in Reagan's transformation was a writer named Suzanne Massie. Massie had become deeply involved with Soviet society at a time when contact between Americans and Russians was unusual. In 1972 she published a book on five poets she had gotten to know in Leningrad, one of whom was Joseph Brodsky, the future Nobel Prize winner. The political contacts she made trying to get a visa to go back to the Soviet Union led her all the way to Reagan. Massie became the president's Russian culture coach and a back channel to the Soviet leadership. She taught Reagan a Russian proverb that he would repeat to the point of Gorbachev's annoyance: *doveryai no proveryai*. "Trust, but verify."

More significant—and the reason Reagan invited her to the White House seventeen times after their initial meeting—was the way Massie bolstered his instincts about "Ivan and Anya," the imaginary Russian couple he evoked in his 1984 speech to the nation. If Shultz dragged the bureaucracy into alignment with Reagan's views, Massie humanized the enemy for him, teaching him always to distinguish the great-souled Russians from the dingy Soviets. Reagan immersed himself in her book *In the Land of the Firebird*, at one point asking Paul Nitze, his chief arms control negotiator, what had happened to entrepreneurial energy represented by the St. Petersburg shopkeepers of 1830. The feeling Massie conveyed to him about Russia's Orthodox religious sensibility, and its persistence in the Soviet era, struck another chord. "She's the greatest student I know of the Russian people," he wrote in his diary. "She's convinced the Russians are going through a spiritual revival & are completely tuned out on Communism."

· · ·

The fifty-four-year-old Gorbachev was well educated and had traveled extensively in the West. He understood English, he wasn't dying, and he even appeared to have a sense of humor. His wife, Raisa, was often at his side, like an American First Lady. In his initial months in power, Gorbachev announced a unilateral freeze on deploying intermediate-range missiles in Europe and began speaking in public about the need for perestroika, economic reform. Kissinger, Nixon, and others gave Reagan their opinion that Gorbachev represented no change at all. But Margaret Thatcher disagreed. "I like Mr. Gorbachev. We can do business together," she told the BBC after meeting him for the first time. Thatcher bolstered Reagan's optimism about the Soviet leader when she visited him at Camp David and delivered a more detailed assessment, warning him, however, that "the more charming the adversary, the more dangerous."

Gorbachev's situation paralleled Reagan's in several ways. He, too, wanted to serve as an agent of societal and political transformation, taking on the alcoholism rampant in Soviet society as well as its faltering economy. Like Reagan, he relied on his own experience more than upon the bureaucratic apparatus beneath him. He shared Reagan's aversion to the logic of mutually assured destruction. Around the same time that Reagan told Soviet foreign minister Andrei Gromyko he wanted to eliminate nuclear weapons, Gorbachev said the same thing in a speech in London. And where Reagan had Shultz to encourage his evolution, Gorbachev had Eduard Shevardnadze, whom he selected to replace Gromyko as foreign minister.

The chief obstacle to the relationship Reagan wanted with the new Soviet leader was the fantasy he cherished. In the run-up to their summit meeting in November 1985, the first meeting of U.S. and Soviet leaders in six years, Gorbachev sent Reagan a letter proposing a 50 percent cut in ICBMs, contingent on a complete ban on space weapons. In negotiating sessions with McFarlane and Shultz, Gorbachev went even further: if the United States gave up the militarization of space, he would be willing to reduce all nuclear forces to zero. Shultz now realized how frightened the Soviets were of SDI, which depended upon technology they didn't know how to develop but knew they could not afford. Like McFarlane, he saw missile defense as a crucial bargaining chip to trade for Soviet concessions.

What Shultz did not yet realize was that Reagan would under no circumstances give it up. Although it had yet to be successfully invented, Reagan viewed SDI as the key to realizing his dream of eliminating nuclear weapons. "We believe that it is important to explore the technical feasibility of defensive systems which might ultimately give all of us the means to protect our people more safely than do those we have at present, and to provide the means of moving to the total abolition of nuclear weapons, an objective on which we are agreed," he wrote to Gorbachev on April 30, 1985. "I must ask you, how are we ever practically to achieve that noble aim if nations have no defense against the uncertainty that all nuclear weapons might not have been removed from world arsenals? Life provides no guarantee against some future madman getting his hands on nuclear weapons."

At their first meeting in Geneva, Reagan proposed that Gorbachev and he throw away their scripts and get to know each other. "You and I were born in small towns about which nobody's ever heard and no one ever expected anything of either of us," he said. The two of them, he pointed out, had the power to destroy the world or make peace. That task might be easier, Reagan said, "if there was a threat to this world from some other species, from another planet, outside the universe." When this comment was publicly reported, some drew a connection to the 1951 sci-fi film *The Day the Earth Stood Still*, in which aliens threaten to destroy the world if earthlings don't rid themselves of nuclear weapons. Gorbachev, twenty years younger, tried to butter up Reagan by sharing some of the anti-Soviet jokes he'd heard the president enjoyed and by noting that he, too, was raised by a mother who read him the Bible.

This, along with his use of phrases such as "God bless" and "if it's God's will" left Reagan gripped by the fancy that Gorbachev could be a secret Christian. Might these phrases mean that he was a believer, he asked Massie?

Reagan craved a "urinal moment," the image he carried in his head from his days at the Screen Actors Guild, when breakthroughs in contract negotiations sometimes took place by way of informal conversations in the men's room. During the afternoon session, he proposed that he and Gorbachev take a walk outside. The two leaders strolled to a pool house by the lake, where a roaring fire awaited. Once inside, Reagan took out a paper and handed it to Gorbachev. It proposed a 50 percent overall cut in nuclear weapons and the elimination of intermediate-range missiles in Europe. Gorbachev studied it and responded, "That's acceptable." But, he said, it wouldn't be possible to proceed with limitations on offensive weapons without an agreement on weapons in space. Where Reagan saw missile defense as a key, Gorbachev regarded it as a lock that made nuclear disarmament impossible. The president's response was that he was prepared to share the technology with the Soviets. But Gorbachev scoffed at this notion, as did Reagan's own negotiating team.

The two remained at loggerheads through the next day, but forged a testy bond. Defying his agreed-upon brief, Reagan invited Gorbachev to make his first visit to the United States the following year. Gorbachev promptly accepted, and reciprocated with an invitation to the USSR the year after that, which Reagan also accepted. "Gorbachev was tough and convinced Communism was superior to capitalism, but after almost five years, I'd finally met a Soviet leader I could talk to," Reagan later wrote. Gorbachev also appreciated the significance of their mutual desire to keep talking, although he regarded Reagan as a "political dinosaur" and had trouble reconciling the American's contradictory statements. The correspondence that followed had a markedly different tone from any Reagan had received from Gorbachev's predecessors. "Mr. President, I would like for you to view my letter as another of our 'fireside chats,'" Gorbachev wrote on December 24, 1985. "I sincerely would like not only to keep the warmth of our Geneva meetings but also move further in development of our dialog. I look at correspondence with you as the most important channel in preparing for our meeting in Washington."

Over the next year, a remarkable transformation took place as Gorbachev and Reagan became jointly enraptured with the idea of ending the balance of terror, and pursued it over near-universal objection inside their own governments. In January 1986, Gorbachev wrote Reagan with a proposal: eliminate all nuclear weapons by 2000. "Why wait until the year 2000?" Reagan responded to aides in the Oval Office. Weinberger and Casey, who had done their best to sabotage the Geneva summit, kill SALT II, and break out of the ABM Treaty, were appalled. Few others inside the Reagan administration took the idea of nuclear abolition seriously. Shultz did. He ordered the State Department's arms control group to get to work on the question of "what a world without nuclear weapons would mean to us" and how to get there. "I know that many of you and others around here oppose the objective of eliminating nuclear weapons, but the president of the United States doesn't agree with you, and he has said so on several very public occasions," he told his colleagues. After much back-and-forth, Weinberger and Shultz were able to agree on a proposal to eliminate ballistic missiles, which Reagan sent to Gorbachev in July 1986.

The calamitous accident at the Chernobyl nuclear reactor in April 1986 intensified Gorbachev's antinuclear feelings and left him all the more eager for an agreement. So, too, did the Soviet Union's deteriorating economic situation. In the fall of 1985, Saudi Arabia announced plans to increase oil production. By the spring of 1986 the world price of oil plummeted from more than thirty dollars a barrel to less than ten. Without hard-currency oil revenues, there was no way for the Soviets to pay for imports of grain and other basic commodities while servicing their foreign debt and keeping up militarily. "The United States has an interest in keeping the negotiations machine running idle, while the arms race overburdens our economy," Gorbachev told a colleague. "That is why we need a breakthrough; we need the process to start moving." In September 1986, Gorbachev wrote Reagan offering a number of unilateral concessions and proposing a meeting ahead of his planned visit to the United States the following year. Shultz encouraged Reagan to meet Gorbachev in Reykjavik, Iceland, the following month.

As the relationship blossomed, Reagan began to appreciate that regardless of Gorbachev's intentions the Soviet Union had become too stressed economically to afford new foreign adventures. This resulted in a shift in the Reagan Doctrine toward broader democratic promotion. Later that fall, when the Ferdinand Marcos dictatorship in the Philippines collapsed, Reagan yielded to Shultz's arguments that the fall of an authoritarian regime might not lead axiomatically to a Communist takeover. However, he didn't apply that logic to South Africa, where his policy remained one of "constructive engagement," pressuring the white apartheid regime to liberalize while opposing the African National Congress because of its Soviet ties. In one of his radio addresses, Reagan made the absurd claim that South African reformers had eliminated segregation, just as the United States had. When Congress passed a comprehensive sanctions bill in 1986, he vetoed it, and Congress overrode his veto.

The new era of improving superpower relations almost came to an end in the fall of 1986, when FBI agents arrested Gennadi Zakharov, a Soviet spy working for the United Nations, on a New York subway platform. A week later, the Soviets retaliated by arresting Nicholas Daniloff, a reporter for *U.S. News and World Report* in Moscow. The KGB had set up Daniloff by getting him to pass a letter from a fake religious dissident to the American ambassador. The incident echoed the Korean airliner shootdown in 1983. Reagan declared Daniloff's arrest "an outrage" and swore he wouldn't swap a journalist hostage for a spy. He was further infuriated when Gorbachev refused to accept his personal assurance that Daniloff had "no connection whatever with the U.S. Government." Republicans were demanding that Shultz refuse to meet with Shevardnadze, who was on his way to Washington for talks.

Despite the harshness of his rhetoric, Reagan's humane instinct and talent for abiding contradictions again proved decisive. His private response to the plight of an American held unjustly didn't match his public one, and he agreed to an exchange that Shultz and

Shevardnadze worked out. On the day he approved it, Reagan wrote in his diary, "This does not mean a trade. This we will not do. Their man is a spy caught red handed and Daniloff is a hostage." The deal was strongly criticized by conservatives. It was, however, a necessity in order to allow the meeting in Iceland to proceed.

Gorbachev arrived at Reykjavik intending to put a significant disarmament package on the table, contingent on Reagan's agreement to slow down the development of space weapons. In fact, Gorbachev's proposal was essentially the one Reagan had originally proposed in Geneva: a 50 percent cut in the ICBMs that were the core of the Soviet nuclear arsenal, and the total elimination of intermediate-range missiles in Europe. To obtain this, Gorbachev was willing to treat limited research on space-based missile defense as compatible with the ABM Treaty. The United States had only to agree to confine its SDI research to the laboratory for ten years, and commit not to withdraw from the ABM Treaty for five years after that.

Over dinner with his advisers, Reagan returned to the even more sweeping idea that he'd raised previously: why not the complete elimination of ballistic missiles? The next day, with Gorbachev, the sky was the limit. When the Americans laid all their ICBMs on the table, Gorbachev called and raised by proposing the elimination of *all* strategic nuclear weapons, including submarines and bombers, over ten years. His bid was still contingent on ten years of adherence to his narrow interpretation of the ABM Treaty, but he indicated he'd be willing to negotiate on that point. This seemingly minor disagreement about how long Star Wars research would stay confined to the laboratory blocked what would have been the most sweeping arms control agreement in history. Knowing his own bottom line and grasping Gorbachev's, Reagan realized that they could go no further. The meeting, so close to a momentous transformation, ended when the president got up and walked out with Shultz while Gorbachev was still decrying the destabilizing effects of SDI.

"This meeting is over," he said. "Let's go, George."

"Can't we do something about this?" Gorbachev pleaded.

"It's too late," Reagan replied.

14

The Facts Tell Me

From the time of Reagan's first election, Nicaragua had preoccupied the president. With the Sandinista leaders aligning themselves with Fidel Castro and supporting leftist rebels in neighboring El Salvador, Reagan worried that the entire region was on the brink of turning red, presaging the "overripe fruit" prophecy. "There is no question but that all of Central Am. is targeted for a Communist takeover," he wrote in his diary after a November 1981 NSC meeting at which he agreed to a plan of covert action to counteract Cuban interference.

The problem of resetting the fallen domino belonged to William Casey at the CIA. Casey had spent the Second World War serving under the father of American intelligence, Wild Bill Donovan, as Donovan's deputy for secret intelligence in Europe. After a career as a corporate lawyer and economic policy maker, he was back to pursuing his original passion on behalf of a president who passionately believed in it himself. In the post–Church Committee world, the CIA was no longer allowed to assassinate foreign leaders or fight secret wars. But Casey took the view that whatever wasn't explicitly prohibited was permitted—and that much of what was prohibited was permissible, too. With Reagan's authorization, the CIA began arming and training the Contras at camps in Honduras.

This placed the administration on a collision path with Democrats who supported a negotiated solution in Nicaragua. In late

1982, Congress passed the Boland Amendment, prohibiting the CIA and Pentagon from spending funds to overthrow the Sandinistas. The administration responded with an end run through a gray area: raising private money to arm the Contras. At the NSC, Bud McFarlane and his deputy, marine lieutenant colonel Oliver North, began soliciting funds from wealthy Republican donors and from friendly foreign governments, including Israel, Taiwan, and Saudi Arabia. The administration crossed other lines as well. In early 1984 the navy mined Nicaragua's harbors. Exhibiting his contempt for Congress's role in foreign policy, Casey misled the intelligence committees of both houses about this act of war. When he found out the truth, Daniel Patrick Moynihan resigned as chairman of the Senate intelligence committee in protest. Congress retaliated with a second, strengthened Boland Amendment. Reagan couldn't understand why Democrats opposed his policy in Nicaragua. He thought Tip O'Neill was pursuing a personal vendetta in blocking a vote on military aid to the Contras.

The Boland Amendment left Casey and McFarlane in a quandary. How could they support the Contras if Congress had passed a law saying they couldn't? This is where North's creativity came into play. A seemingly ingenuous patriot, North had a delusional streak. He told stories about his relationship with Reagan that no one believed. The intersection of North's fantasies and Reagan's fog would later make the events of 1985 and 1986 almost impossible to untangle. But as the story eventually emerged, North was by this time raising large sums in secret, and using them at his discretion for what was now a clearly illegal Contra-resupply operation. The accounting for these off-the-books funds was haphazard at best. Elliott Abrams, the undersecretary of state for Latin America, lost ten million dollars that the Sultan of Brunei donated by transposing the numbers of a secret offshore bank account. Other money was stolen. Richard Secord, a retired air force general, used Swiss bank accounts to buy himself a plane and a Porsche, and to pay for a fifteen-thousand-dollar security fence for North's house in Virginia.

In his second term, Reagan became as fixated on saving seven

Americans Hezbollah had taken hostage in Lebanon as he was by supporting the Contras. This preoccupation emerged from a wave of terrorist attacks and reprisals that began with the hijacking of TWA Flight 847 in June 1985. The plane was on its way from Athens to Rome when Lebanese hijackers forced it to land in Beirut. There they threw the body of a murdered navy diver onto the tarmac and held captive the rest of the passengers, most of them Americans. The captors demanded the release of several hundred prisoners in Israeli jails. After a long ordeal, the passengers were released.

The episode left Reagan gripped by the desire to punish sponsors of terrorism—the name he came back to most often was Libya's Muammar Gaddafi—and obsessed with freeing the seven Americans held in Beirut. "It just drove him crazy," Shultz recalled. "There were these hostages in Lebanon, Americans being tortured, and he couldn't do anything about it, and he's their president." A paradox of Reagan's mentality is what I've called his inversion layer, that he stayed aloof in relationships with others, but felt his way through abstract issues by making them into stories about individual people. As he'd demonstrated in Grenada, Reagan saw the protection of American citizens abroad as a primary obligation. This lifeguard bias underpinned the Iran-Contra scandal, which was driven by his desperation to rescue hostages with names and faces at the expense of nameless future victims. In public, Reagan's position was that terrorists must be hunted down and punished, not negotiated with. In private, he readily opened his checkbook to free captive Americans.

Reagan's obsession with the hostages set the stage for what happened next. David Kimche, the director-general of Israel's foreign affairs ministry, suggested to McFarlane that the United States might obtain Iranian help with the hostages held by its Hezbollah allies by supplying spare parts for American military equipment left over from the shah. Israel's interest was in tipping the Iran-Iraq seesaw away from Iraq, which appeared in the 1980s as the greater threat. The conduit Kimche proposed was a dodgy Iranian arms dealer named Manucher Ghorbanifar, who claimed to be in touch with elusive Iranian "moderates." As it later turned out, the CIA knew Ghorbanifar was basically a fraud.

That summer, a colonoscopy turned up a polyp on Reagan's colon, and doctors scheduled him for abdominal surgery the next day. McFarlane insisted on going to see Reagan in the hospital while he was still recovering, to propose an explicit trade of TOW missiles for American hostages. McFarlane warned Reagan that the sale, brokered through the Israelis, would probably be illegal. "I want to find a way to do this," Reagan told him. He would subsequently press McFarlane to pursue the trade over the objections of Shultz and Weinberger, who despite their mutual antipathy agreed that it was a terrible idea to simultaneously countermand so many American policies: the ban on arms sales to Iran, neutrality in the Iran-Iraq War, and the prohibition on negotiating with terrorists. Casey, however, was enthusiastic about the scheme.

Given Reagan's disconnectedness, many people later assumed that manipulative aides had enlisted him in their agenda. But Reagan was the one hooked on hostage fishing. "I don't think I could forgive myself if we didn't try," Admiral John Poindexter, who would succeed McFarlane as national security adviser, recalled the president saying. After the first transfer of TOW antitank missiles, the release of one of the hostages, Benjamin Weir, in August 1985 encouraged Reagan to press on. He phoned Weir from Air Force One to express his relief and say he wouldn't rest until the six others were freed. Emotional meetings with the families of hostages motivated him further. "Okay, what are we doing to get my hostages?" he would ask at the end of national security briefings.

McFarlane took the signal to sell bigger and better HAWK surface-to-air missiles to the Iranians. Reagan kept pushing McFarlane not to give up, even after his national security adviser resigned from exhaustion, and even after a humiliating secret mission to Iran, where McFarlane traveled with North under assumed identities with fake Irish passports supplied by the CIA. The two came bearing gifts: pallets of TOW missiles, six .357 Magnum handguns in presentation cases, a Bible with a verse inscribed by the president, and a chocolate cake in the shape of a key, to symbolize the opening of relations, from a kosher bakery in Tel Aviv. They expected to meet with the speaker of the Iranian parliament and to leave with a promise to free the remaining hostages. Instead, McFarlane saw only underlings, who complained that they'd been overcharged for previous weapons shipments. Islamic Revolutionary Corps guards at the airport ate the cake.

After McFarlane stepped down, Poindexter took charge of the arms transfers to Iran. In January 1986, Reagan signed a secret finding authorizing further sales. Poindexter advised him to exercise his "statutory prerogative" to withhold notification from Congress. When a second prisoner, Father Lawrence Jenco, was released almost a year after the first, Reagan read it as a "delayed step in a plan we've been working on," and sent more missiles as a thank-you present. Two other hostages would be released when U.S. officials threatened to cut off the flow of weapons, but an additional six were eventually taken—a net loss of two, in exchange for 2,008 missiles. In 1985 and 1986, Reagan knew he was trading arms for hostages, but seems not to have understood how poorly the operation was going.

. . .

Oliver North's "neat idea," approved by Poindexter, was to redirect proceeds from the Iranian arms sales to the Contras, to supplement private and third-country donations. He later claimed to have spelled out the plan in five memos to the president. Only one of those memos, the April 4, 1986, "diversion memo," survived the shredder, and there has never been clear evidence that Reagan saw it or any others that may have existed. The scheme turned out to be as unnecessary as it was illegal. In June 1986, Reagan persuaded Congress to reverse its rejection of $100 million in aid for the Contras, making irrelevant the $3.8 million North was able to filch for them from the Iranian arms sales.

The unraveling came quickly, in the fall of 1986. Covert support for the Contras was exposed in October, when one of the pilots working for Richard Secord's resupply operation was shot

down over Nicaragua and captured with a black book of phone
numbers. A few weeks later, the Lebanese newspaper *Al Shiraa*
reported that the United States was sending spare parts for American weapons to Iran. Revelations about McFarlane's secret trip and
arms-for-hostages dealings followed. On November 13, Reagan
went on television to deny that his administration had been sending weapons to Iran or making deals with terrorists. At a disastrous
press conference six days later, he took back his denial about the
missile transfers but still insisted he had not traded arms for hostages. He continued to evade what he'd done with diminishing
coherence, blaming the press for putting the hostages in danger.

Washington was now asking the old question: What did the
president know, and when did he know it? Attorney General Edwin
Meese led the internal investigation, a task he approached not as
the nation's chief law enforcement officer but as Reagan's confi-
dant. On November 23, Justice Department attorneys found
North's diversion memo and learned that the U.S. government had
received only twelve million of the thirty million dollars paid by
the Iranians. Meese took no steps to secure evidence of what now
looked like a crime. North spent the night in his office destroying
documents with his secretary, Fawn Hall. They worked the shred-
ders so hard the machines broke down. At that point, North walked
to the White House Situation Room to make use of the shredder
there. Hall spirited out other incriminating papers by stuffing
them down the front of her blouse and into her boots. North and
Poindexter also attempted to erase thousands of electronic messages on an internal communications system.

Reagan didn't exhibit any knowledge about the diversion in
public or private. "North didn't tell me about this. Worst of all,
John P. found out about it and didn't tell me. This may call for
resignations," Reagan wrote in his diary on November 24. The next
day, Reagan announced North's dismissal and Poindexter's resignation, claiming that he "was not fully informed of the nature of
one of the activities undertaken in connection with this initiative,"
then leaving the Briefing Room so Meese could explain what he
was talking about. But Reagan did not treat North like someone

who had betrayed him. The president phoned his motel room in Vienna, Virginia, to thank him and call him a hero.

As the scandal metastasized, Reagan appointed a commission, led by Senator John Tower, to investigate. Meese then appointed Lawrence Walsh, a New York City lawyer with a reputation for rectitude, as an independent prosecutor. Investigations four and five began separately in the House and Senate, and were later combined. During the joint congressional hearings that began in May 1987, North cast himself as a can-do patriot willing to lie, cheat, and steal for his country. The pipe-smoking Poindexter was, by contrast, a colorless bureaucrat, spontaneously afflicted by a failing memory. "The buck stops here with me. I made the decision," Poindexter testified to Congress about the diversion. "I felt that I had the authority to do it. I was convinced that the President would, in the end, think it was a good idea. But I didn't want him to be associated with the decision." The only other person who might know the truth was Casey, and he wasn't sharing it, either. The day before he was to testify to the Senate panel, he was hospitalized for what turned out to be a malignant brain tumor, and he died several months later. McFarlane came across as the most sympathetic figure in the scandal. Overwhelmed by the pressures of his job and believing he had failed his country, he swallowed an overdose of Valium, but survived.

North was indicted on sixteen felony counts and convicted of three, including accepting an illegal gratuity and ordering the destruction of documents. He was given a suspended sentence, fines, and community service. Despite considerable pressure from the right, Reagan declined to pardon him during his final days in office. North's convictions were later vacated by an appeals court on grounds related to his grant of congressional immunity. Poindexter's conviction on five counts of lying and obstruction was reversed on the same grounds. McFarlane pled guilty to four misdemeanor counts of withholding information from Congress, and was sentenced to two years' probation, but was pardoned by President George H. W. Bush. In 1992 the implacable Walsh belatedly indicted Caspar Weinberger on two counts of perjury, but Bush pardoned him as well, concluding what had become a grudge match among ancients.

The joint congressional report concluded that North and the others had acted as a secret cabal inside the administration following what they believed to be Reagan's wishes. "When exposure was threatened, they destroyed official documents, lied to Cabinet officials, to the public, and to elected representatives in Congress," the report said. Left unanswered was the question of the president's culpability. In January 1987, Reagan had prostate surgery, which took him out of circulation for several weeks and left him more muddled than before. Asking him about his previous knowledge had all the impact of penetrating a dense mist with a sharp stick. In his first interview with the Tower Commission, Reagan said he had first authorized shipments of arms from Israel to Iran in 1985. But after consulting with his chief of staff, he asked to revise his testimony to say that he hadn't known about them until 1986. During his second session, he answered questions by reading directly from his briefing memo: "If the question comes up at the Tower meeting, you might want to say that you were surprised." Afterward, he wrote to Tower to correct himself again. "The only honest answer is to state that try as I might, I cannot recall anything whatsoever about whether I approved a replenishment of Israeli stocks around August of 1985," he said.

Reagan had suffered from convenient memory lapses before, most notably in his 1962 grand jury testimony about SAG giving MCA the "blanket waiver." In that instance as well, faulty memory was the mechanism by which he absolved himself for doing something that violated his principles. But there was a meaningful difference between Reagan's self-protective blur at age fifty-one and at age seventy-six, when even his severest critics didn't accuse him of intentional deception. The Tower Commission, which held Reagan responsible but depicted him as not understanding what was going on, vouched for the genuineness of his confusion.

Reagan's March 4, 1987, television address, in which he accepted the Tower Commission's conclusions, supported that determination. "A few months ago," he said, "I told the American people that

I did not trade arms for hostages. My heart and my best intentions still tell me that's true, but the facts and the evidence tell me it is not." Reagan never said anything more revealing about his psyche. Confronted by his transgression, he acknowledged reality, but as a separate department without the authority to compromise his identity as a moral person.

How could Reagan both know and not know he was trading arms for hostages? And what was his responsibility if he had known, but no longer knew that he had known? Given the apparent onset of mental decline around the same time, the issue of his culpability becomes a hopeless epistemological conundrum. In 2015, researchers at Arizona State University published a study in the *Journal of Alzheimer's Disease* comparing Reagan's use of language in presidential press conferences to that of George H. W. Bush. "President Reagan showed a significant reduction in the number of unique words over time and a significant increase in conversational fillers and non-specific nouns over time," the researchers wrote. "There was no significant trend in these features for President Bush." Reagan's diaries, which are numbingly repetitive and tedious at their best, become painfully mechanical around 1987. "I have three things to tell you," he kidded with Dr. Lawrence Mohr, his White House physician that year. "The first is that I seem to be having a little trouble with my memory. I can't remember the other two."

After his speech, Reagan took the same position on Iran-Contra that he had toward Watergate: it was time for the country to move on. But the scandal, which took over his presidency for many months, exacted a heavy toll. As he wrote after leaving office, "For the first time in my life, people didn't believe me." Between October 1986 and March 1987, Reagan's approval rating fell twenty points, to 43 percent, a number not seen since the depths of the 1981–82 recession. Nancy blamed Don Regan, who she thought should be fired for failing to protect the president as the troika had. After telling her husband that the chief of staff had hung up the phone on her, she got her wish. Before Reagan could offer Regan a dignified resignation, the First Lady's office leaked word that the former Senate majority leader Howard Baker would be replacing him. It was shabby treatment after six years of loyal service.

• • •

The president's diminished position showed in October 1987, when the Senate rejected his nomination of Robert Bork to replace Lewis Powell on the Supreme Court. That same month, the stock market crashed, with the Dow falling 22.6 percent in a single day. It was a personal low point for Reagan as well. After being diagnosed with breast cancer, Nancy underwent a double mastectomy. During the surgery, Reagan broke down crying in the waiting room.

His presidency in a kind of tailspin, Reagan tried again by nominating Douglas Ginsburg, a federal court of appeals judge, who soon withdrew his name from consideration following reports that he had smoked marijuana as a student and young law professor. It might not have mattered if Nancy Reagan hadn't made "Just Say No" to drugs her pet cause, or if the moralizing secretary of education William Bennett hadn't pushed for Ginsburg to bow out. After those two misses, Reagan was finally successful in his nomination of Anthony Kennedy, whose views were more moderate than doctrinaire conservatives would have liked. Kennedy would later join O'Connor in recognizing a constitutional right to abortion in the 1992 case *Planned Parenthood v. Casey*. Of Reagan's three Supreme Court appointments, only Antonin Scalia would consistently please conservatives.

Following Iran-Contra, the administration's residual policy agenda ebbed away. As officials began to position themselves for life after the White House, the prevailing mentality inside the administration became one of every man for himself. Reagan's lack of suspiciousness and his disconnection from the details of governing created an atmosphere where ethical lines were blurred and often crossed. His former aide Michael Deaver become a high-priced lobbyist and was later indicted by a federal grand jury for lying to a House committee. Deaver was later convicted on three counts and sentenced to probation, community service, and a large fine.

Another former aide, Lyn Nofziger, was prosecuted for similar infractions and in 1988 was convicted on three counts and sentenced to ninety days in prison, based on his lobbying of Edwin Meese on behalf of Wedtech and other clients. An appeals court later reversed Nofziger's convictions based on a technicality.

Another special prosecutor was appointed to investigate Meese himself for violating conflict-of-interest rules in the Wedtech case. Meese had helped Wedtech secure $250 million in no-bid defense contracts based on its fraudulent status as a minority-owned business. Instead of indicting Meese, the special prosecutor wrote a report attacking his ethics. Meese played it the same way Reagan had with Iran-Contra: he pled obliviousness. Facing a further investigation by the Justice Department's Office of Professional Responsibility, he resigned in July 1988.

Moralistic in other areas, Reagan sent no signals to his staff about the integrity of government decision making. His hostility toward Washington combined with the celebration of entrepreneurship to breed acceptance for the exploitation of public offices for private gain. People who had suffered public-sector salaries to fight against the bureaucracy came to regard manipulating it on behalf of paying clients as a kind of postemployment perk. In keeping with this ethos, 1980s Washington came to revolve around the pursuit of wealth in a way it had not for many previous decades. Lobbyist-for-hire went from being a furtive, disreputable job to one that people boasted about.

The president's reflexive support for his people encouraged these attitudes. When negative stories emerged, Reagan dismissed them as politically driven or expressions of a lynch mob mentality on the part of the media. He never entertained the possibility that those loyal to him would do things that were improper, or that he himself might have contributed to an atmosphere of corruption. But in combination with Iran-Contra, the parade of aides in legal trouble left the feeling that goods were walking out the door while the watchman dozed.

Often quite literally. That summer, Reagan was due to return to the Vatican to meet once more with the pope. Five years after his embarrassing 1982 incident, his staff was determined not to let him fall asleep again. He and Nancy arrived in Italy several days early. A bed they found especially comfortable was flown in from Portugal. The Reagans spent several days acclimating to the time zone, relaxing, and watching movies. But the president was no match for the sonorous tone of the pontiff's voice. Seeing what was happening, the White House photographer deliberately dropped his camera. It clattered on the Vatican's marble floor, reawakening the president.

15

Tear Down This Wall

As the limousines pulled away in Reykjavik in October 1986, both sides felt immense disappointment. In retrospect, the near deal would come to be seen as the Cold War's turning point, but at the time it was experienced as an impasse. Gorbachev went back to the Politburo and denounced Reagan as a class enemy, a primitive, and a caveman. In Washington, Shultz blamed Gorbachev for letting the agreement fall through. Others blamed Shultz for letting Reagan get his back up over an insignificant delay in SDI testing.

Did Reagan walk out on Gorbachev because he sensed that he was teetering on the edge of a catastrophic success, that after capturing so many imaginations he needed to return to reality? Both the near deal and its collapse had elements of the absurd about them. Reagan had come to cherish two fantasies and put them on a collision course. The first fantasy was abolishing nuclear weapons. The second was replacing those weapons with an impregnable shield. Neither was remotely plausible. Four other countries possessed their own nuclear forces. It was far-fetched to think that the Soviet Union would disarm if China didn't; or that France, Britain, and Israel would relinquish their nuclear deterrents. Could such a sweeping treaty possibly be verified? Could it pass the U.S. Senate?

The second fantasy was the Strategic Defense Initiative. Over the subsequent ten years, the United States never exceeded the "narrow" definition of the ABM Treaty that Gorbachev held on to as his bottom line in Reykjavik. Despite lavish funding, research produced very little. The Defense Department never had any X-ray lasers, "brilliant pebbles," or other space-based technology to test outside a laboratory. In 1993 the Pentagon abandoned the pursuit of space-based missile defense in favor of more practical ground-based interception systems to deal with the "madman" risk Reagan often cited.

It may seem preposterous that this never-developed technology was such an alarming prospect to Gorbachev. The physicists who accompanied him to Reykjavik told him that an impenetrable nuclear shield was technologically unrealistic. But Reagan's will was a powerful force in world affairs. The technical obstacles to what he called his "dream" neither bothered nor interested him. Reagan got Gorbachev to believe in his inertia projector by believing in it so fervently himself. The fear of an imaginary defensive weapon, and the dawning recognition of Reagan's absolute refusal to relinquish or rein it in, propelled Gorbachev's recognition that continued military competition with the United States had become infeasible. Thus did the Cold War pivot from mutually assured destruction to mutually supported magical thinking.

There was a break of several months in Gorbachev's correspondence with Reagan, during which the Soviet leader stewed over Reykjavik and the White House was consumed with Iran-Contra. But in the spring of 1987, both leaders wanted a deal more than ever. In the Soviet Union, perestroika had raised expectations but yielded little in the way of economic betterment. This led Gorbachev to accelerate modernization and seek compromise. He freed dozens of political prisoners and announced a withdrawal from Afghanistan. He also offered unilateral concessions on arms control: a moratorium on nuclear testing and a new doctrine that forswore offensive military action or expansionist ambitions. What Jack Matlock calls Reagan's "transparency of intent" encouraged Gorbachev to treat the president's desire for peace as sincere. He tried harder to accommodate Reagan's commitment to missile defense, dropping his insistence that research be limited to the laboratory as a condition of a treaty on intermediate-range nuclear missiles.

Reagan, too, was eager for an arms control deal to restore his stature after Iran-Contra. In April, Americans discovered that the Soviets had obtained access to the U.S. embassy in Moscow through a marine guard whose girlfriend was working undercover for the KGB. Weinberger, who tried to make Reagan think the Soviets already had a version of SDI, seized upon the incident as another opportunity to scuttle negotiations. Conservatives demanded that Shultz cancel a planned trip to Moscow. Instead, Reagan sent a personal letter saying that while he felt strongly about the violation of the embassy, he was encouraged by other steps Gorbachev was taking.

Reagan saw no conflict between this kind of private conciliation and public confrontation. He regarded moral pressure as a powerful lever in ongoing negotiations. On a trip to Berlin that spring, Reagan spoke at the Brandenburg Gate, where the Soviets had divided the East from the West. He acknowledged movement toward reform while proclaiming, "Mr. Gorbachev, open this gate! Mr. Gorbachev, tear down this wall!" The words were Reagan's own, and he had resisted pressure to remove them from the speech. Until nearly the end of his presidency, he remained an outlier in his belief that the Soviet Union could change.

The speech wasn't merely superb political theater. It helped shore up Reagan's position with a right wing skeptical about his newfound enthusiasm for arms control. The treaty on intermediate-range nuclear forces, which was concluded in September 1987, required the destruction of all missiles with a range of 300 to 3,400 miles, some 2,611 in total. Realists such as Nixon and Kissinger thought that Reagan had either lost his marbles or was making a historic mistake out of desperation to appear as a peacemaker in his final years in office. Reagan supporters such as George Will and Charles Krauthammer attacked the treaty as disastrous capitulation. William F. Buckley called it a "suicide pact." Robert Dole, the Senate minority leader, accused the president of "stuffing this treaty down the throats of our allies."

His cabinet was hardly more enthusiastic. Of his pre-scandal national security team, only Shultz remained by the end of 1987. Frank Carlucci had replaced Weinberger as secretary of defense. Colin Powell was the new national security adviser, Reagan's sixth in seven years. William Webster took Casey's spot at the CIA. These new players didn't support either of the president's pet ideas, nuclear abolition or SDI, both of which they saw as undermining deterrence. "Howard, I think I'm the only person left in this government who wants to try to see the completion of an INF Treaty with the Soviets," Reagan told his new chief of staff Howard Baker.

In the end, not much presidential lobbying was necessary. Despite a filibuster from Senators Dan Quayle and Jesse Helms, the INF Treaty was ratified by a vote of 93–5. The signing was to take place during Gorbachev's visit to Washington on December 8, 1987, at 1:45 p.m., based on one of Joan Quigley's horoscopes. Publicly, the visit marked the transformation of superpower relations. Gorbachev charmed his way through the nation's capital, which received him as a global celebrity. Behind the scenes, Reagan was driving his Soviet guest crazy with his constant repetition of *doveryai no proveryai*. The president performed disastrously in a session with Gorbachev and the cabinet, where he rambled semicoherently and told anti-Soviet jokes.

In a meeting the next day, Reagan fared better but failed to appreciate that Gorbachev was essentially offering to concede on the development of missile defense as part of a broader agreement. Reagan and Shultz still wanted a deal on long-range missiles. But the president no longer had enough time left, or sufficient support inside his administration, to negotiate a broader agreement. That spring, another public embarrassment diminished his credibility further, when Donald Regan took his revenge with a hastily constructed memoir. In it, he revealed Nancy's application of astrology to world affairs. In response, the president's powers of denial kicked in once more. Much in the way he had reacted to Iran-Contra, he initially said Regan's account was a pack of falsehoods, before being forced to square his statements with powerful evidence to the contrary.

In May 1988, Reagan finally got to see inside the Soviet Union, at the final summit meeting of his presidency in Moscow. Overriding objections from the KGB, he stopped his limousine so he could get out and see Muscovites taking a Sunday walk along the Arbat. He was appalled when the Russian police roughed up citizens eager for a glimpse of him, and several American reporters along with them. With no arms control agenda left open, Reagan attended to human rights activists and Jewish refuseniks, nearly one hundred of whom he hosted at a dinner at Spaso House, the U.S. ambassador's residence. He asked Gorbachev to make freedom of religion a right, and repeated his request to tear down the wall. "It's time, my friend, it's time," Reagan said, quoting Pushkin.

At dinner the next night, Shultz was unable to keep the president awake while Gorbachev was speaking. Nevertheless, the trip provided the Soviet leader with the personal support he believed crucial to his political survival in the face of a brewing reaction from the old guard. At a press conference, Reagan downplayed his role in the Soviet transformation, saying that it was Gorbachev who deserved most of the credit for the changes under way. As the two leaders walked across Red Square, a reporter asked if he still saw the Soviet Union as the evil empire. "I was talking about another time, another era," Reagan said.

By then, the forces Gorbachev had unleashed were making further arms control negotiations irrelevant. He had intended to modernize the Soviet Union, not destroy it. But as Reagan had long surmised, the system was too fundamentally broken to withstand repair. The dismantling soon took on a logic of its own. A month after the Moscow summit, Gorbachev convened a general conference of the Communist Party, the first of its kind since the Stalin era. The result was a system of genuine elections for the national legislature, and a new elective presidency. Following the conference, he moved swiftly to purge his hard-line opponents.

At the end of 1988, Gorbachev returned to the United States to deliver a speech to the United Nations. There he announced a unilateral reduction of five hundred thousand troops and a withdrawal of most Soviet forces from East Germany, Czechoslovakia, and Hungary. "The use or threat of force no longer can or must be an instrument of foreign policy," he declared. This was widely interpreted as a signal that the Soviet Union would not intervene to keep Eastern Europe under its control. The speech validated Gorbachev's sincerity and Reagan's embrace of him. Afterward, Reagan hosted a lunch for Gorbachev at the U.S. Coast Guard station on Governors Island, with the Statue of Liberty as the backdrop and with his successor, President-elect George H. W. Bush, at his side. Directing his remarks to the incoming president, Gorbachev said, "I'm doing this because I need to. I'm doing this because there's a revolution taking place in my country. I started it."

He had, and it became increasingly clear it couldn't be stopped. "The Cold War is over," Reagan said as he boarded Air Force One, leaving Washington for home after George Bush's inauguration on January 20, 1989. Within a year, the Berlin Wall came down and the nations of Eastern Europe overthrew long-standing dictators and claimed their independence. At the end of 1991, the Soviet Union was formally dissolved.

. . .

Though he lived another fifteen years after leaving office, Reagan was to have no postpresidential act. Riding a horse in Mexico in July 1989, he was thrown off and hit his head. Doctors at the Mayo Clinic who treated him for a buildup of fluid on the brain expressed concern to his family that he might have Alzheimer's disease. Nancy held off telling him for several years, until his forgetfulness became too obvious to deny. In November 1994, Reagan summoned his powers one last time to compose a letter to the nation disclosing his affliction. In a spidery hand, he wrote that he still felt fine, but understood the ordeal Nancy would face in caring for him.

In closing let me thank you, the American people for giving me the great honor of allowing me to serve as your President. When the Lord calls me home, whenever that may be, I will leave with the greatest love for this country of ours and eternal optimism for its future. I now begin the journey that will lead me into the sunset of my life. I know that for America there will always be a bright dawn ahead.

With that, he vanished into the fog. Nancy made sure the country never saw her husband as a diminished force. Ronald Reagan died on June 5, 2004, at the age of ninety-three. He is buried at his presidential library in Simi Valley, California.

Conclusion

That's How I Saw It

Reagan's 1989 farewell address to the nation was a bookend to his "America the Beautiful" speech in Fulton thirty-seven years earlier, when he first articulated his vision of American exceptionalism.

> The past few days when I've been at that window upstairs, I've thought a bit of the "shining city upon a hill." The phrase comes from John Winthrop, who wrote it to describe the America he imagined. What he imagined was important because he was an early Pilgrim, an early freedom man. He journeyed here on what today we'd call a little wooden boat; and like the other Pilgrims, he was looking for a home that would be free. I've spoken of the shining city all my political life, but I don't know if I ever quite communicated what I saw when I said it. But in my mind it was a tall, proud city built on rocks stronger than oceans, windswept, God-blessed, and teeming with people of all kinds living in harmony and peace; a city with free ports that hummed with commerce and creativity. And if there had to be city walls, the walls had doors and the doors were open to anyone with the will and the heart to get here. That's how I saw it, and see it still.

In the period since, American politics has been defined around this ingenuous man and his unclouded vision. We see him now through a fog of our own, a haze of myth that obscures the true picture of what he did and didn't accomplish. Years after his death, we still find it hard to let Reagan be Reagan.

He cast an especially long shadow over the Bush family. George H. W. Bush, his successor, faced the challenge of maintaining Reagan's political coalition while asserting an independent identity. As president he attempted to be "kinder and gentler" on social policy, more fiscally responsible, and in world affairs less righteous and idealistic. This was less a softening of Reaganism than a repudiation of its key features. Conservatives judged Bush harshly for failing to live up to Reagan's example when he agreed to raise taxes in the face of a swelling deficit—though Reagan repeatedly did the same thing without acknowledging it.

Bush's 1992 defeat convinced most Republican politicians that emulating Reagan was the only path to salvation. Eight years later, George W. Bush spurned his father's moderation to claim Reagan's paternity. He managed his administration like a CEO, espoused "moral clarity," and created enormous deficits by cutting taxes while spending lavishly on the military. It's hard to imagine a more literal-minded reenactment. Yet many conservatives judged the second Bush as insufficiently Reaganite because of the way he permitted government to expand.

By the time Bush left office in 2009, the claim that Reagan would have done something differently, or would never have done something, had become an argument ender in GOP circles. Reagan's choice was axiomatically the right one. Republican candidates continue to claim the Gipper's mantle. But what does being like Reagan mean today? The simplest definition might be finding a way to win elections as a conservative. For the GOP, the Reagan years represent success that came from unifying around a leader and a message. Most Republicans also continue to proclaim the views Reagan held. Leaving aside Reagan's liberal stands on immigration and the federal handgun law he supported to honor Jim Brady, nearly all prominent Republicans agree on lowering taxes, reducing the role of the federal government, and making abortion illegal. At a broader level, conservatives understand Reaganism to mean projecting optimism, expressing patriotism, and speaking unashamedly about morality. Reagan's disciples extol "American exceptionalism" and allege that their liberal opponents don't believe in it.

Democrats, too, believe Reagan is a worthy model in many respects. They aspire to emulate his leadership qualities, his positive outlook, and his ambitious goals in office. Democratic political consultants spout the same clichés as their Republican counterparts about the need for leaders to be forward-looking (though Reagan was deeply nostalgic), to bring factions together (though Reagan challenged his own party from the right), and to be clear in their beliefs (though Reagan's were filled with contradictions). In 1992, Bill Clinton mimicked aspects of Reagan's style as he unified a party with disparate views and applied moralistic language to social policy. During the 2008 primaries, Barack Obama was more explicit in pointing out his aspiration to be like Reagan, who "changed the trajectory of America in a way that, you know, Richard Nixon did not and in a way that Bill Clinton did not." For Obama, as for George W. Bush, being like Reagan meant being a consequential president. Obama also came to accept the political imperative of proclaiming America's specialness among nations. In 2014 he declared, "I believe in American exceptionalism with every fiber of my being." Obama's speech, a commencement address at West Point, was a kind of dialogue with Reagan's ghost.

Reagan himself never used phrases such as "American exceptionalism" or "moral clarity," any more than he talked about being visionary or consequential. He had a low level of self-consciousness, and expressed these concepts simply by being himself. If none of his successors formed the kind of bond he did with the country, it may be because few politicians have ever embodied the idealized national character the way Reagan did. Simplicity, innocence, and personal modesty are rare qualities in public life, and difficult ones to fake. People excused Reagan's lapses and contradictions because they believed he was genuine and recognized themselves in his aspirations.

Reagan's claim to the nation's affection rests on his American personality: his homespun wit, his good nature, and his native optimism. His claim to greatness rests on his role in the end of the Cold War and the collapse of communism. To put the case in the simplest possible terms, the Soviet Union didn't fall; it was pushed. The push that Gorbachev gave it was the proximate cause, but it reflected pressure that Reagan began to apply four years before Gorbachev came to power. Gorbachev's goal was to reform and strengthen the Soviet Union. Reagan's goal was to render it harmless. Though the shove he gave it came from farther away, it was intended to produce the outcome that followed, one that he was nearly alone in thinking possible.

Reagan's Soviet policy was hard to make sense of while he was in office. His goals of victory over the Soviets, protection from the Soviets, and peace with the Soviets coexisted in unresolved tension. He was intent on diminishing the risk of nuclear catastrophe but came into office with no strategy for doing so. He began by adhering to conservative ideology, and when that failed to produce the result he wanted, he reversed course and followed his gut instead. In the first term, he rejected arms control and participated in no negotiations. That didn't point toward the safer world he wanted, so he changed course, becoming an unexpected apostle of nuclear abolition. Reagan's yearning for a Soviet leader he could work with contradicted his belief that Communists couldn't be trusted. His craving for disarmament stood at odds with his suspicion of treaties.

In retrospect, however, we can see the larger sense of what Reagan was doing, which was lost on both supporters and critics. Reagan began by applying military, moral, and economic pressure to the Soviet Union to force a change in behavior. Before the Soviet Union showed any sign of yielding, he extended an olive branch with his other hand. When Gorbachev responded to this combination of tactics, he embraced the possibility of Soviet transformation. Sensing that Gorbachev needed his help to continue, he lent his personal support. These were improvisations, but on the theme of making the world a safer place. Reagan was often wrong on facts, but his personal instincts usually outshone those of his contemporaries.

The Soviet collapse couldn't have happened without Gorbachev. But it probably would not have happened the way it did without

Reagan, either. What if George H. W. Bush had beaten Reagan in New Hampshire in 1980 and gone on to get elected and reelected, with Reagan becoming his vice president? In all likelihood, Bush would have pursued a realist foreign policy that emphasized stability, shied away from moral posturing, and accepted the Cold War status quo as a permanent condition. The Soviets would have felt no economic pressure from an accelerated arms race or SDI, and no moral pressure from a righteous American leader. Disarmament negotiations might have gotten further in a first term, but would have lacked the world-changing ambition in the second. The economic pressures that helped bring Gorbachev to power in 1985 and forced him to press forward with perestroika might have been reduced or delayed.

Or imagine that Reagan's Alzheimer's had been diagnosed earlier, obliging him to resign after his confused Iran-Contra testimony in 1987. The forces that brought down the Soviet Union were too far along at that point for a change in American leadership to have allowed it to recover. But it's hard to imagine that a President Bush would have seized the opportunity to transform superpower relations in the way Reagan did. Reagan's credibility with conservatives made it politically possible for him to pass the INF Treaty and pursue radical disarmament in a way Bush couldn't have. If only Nixon could go to China, only Reagan could make peace with the Soviet Union.

· · ·

When it comes to domestic governance, Reagan's accomplishments are more contestable. Here, too, he had an enormous goal, which was to reverse the era of government expansion that Franklin Roosevelt began when Reagan was a young man who believed in him during the Great Depression. Into the 1970s, Republican presidents accepted the premises of the twentieth-century liberal project, occasionally slowing the expansion of government but never fundamentally challenging the premise that it was the only way to address society's greatest challenges. Reagan rejected that assumption but did not, as he claimed to have done after the passage of his 1981 budget, "boldly reverse the trend of government." He neither reduced its overall cost nor made significant changes to federalism, eligibility for welfare, or other antipoverty programs. Reagan left behind a federal government that was less ambitious but not smaller or less powerful.

His domestic legacy is the stalemate around the role of government that has persisted since he left office. Attacks on the federal bureaucracy have remained the overarching theme of Republican politics, but they have produced only limited results. The 1994 Contract with America renewed the assault on Washington with a harsher edge. As Speaker of the House, Newt Gingrich aspired to complete the Reagan counterrevolution, much as Truman, Kennedy, and Johnson tried to extend the New Deal. Gingrich, like Reagan, believed that most of the federal government wasn't valuable and that voters wouldn't miss it if it went away. This assumption did not serve him well. The government shutdowns Gingrich provoked in 1995 and 1996 made him deeply unpopular, and helped to reelect Bill Clinton.

Democratic leaders have tried to accommodate Reaganism by acknowledging government's capacity for overreaching. In his 1984 address at the Democratic convention, Mario Cuomo, the most eloquent defender of traditional liberalism, avowed, "We believe in only the government we need, but we insist on all the government we need." In his 1996 State of the Union address, Bill Clinton declared, "The era of big government is over." In this context, the Clinton-Gingrich agreement to eliminate welfare as an entitlement in 1996 might be seen as a postpresidential victory for Reagan. But if so, the passage of the Affordable Care Act in 2010, filling in the biggest missing piece of the liberal welfare state, was a posthumous defeat. Since Reagan, Republicans have learned to challenge government more cautiously even as Democrats have learned that they expand government at their peril.

What Reagan did change was the public's attitude toward government, for better and for worse. Reagan followed a string of presidencies that had fundamentally failed: those of Johnson, Nixon,

Ford, and Carter. Many political scientists came to believe that the job had become impossible: the executive branch was too vast and complex for any one person to manage. Reagan's popularity and accomplishments restored the idea that someone could be successful in the job. At the same time, he enshrined a hypocritical attitude toward Washington: the view that it should cost less but do more. American politics continues to incorporate Reagan's evasion of trade-offs, his message that the country can have it both ways. Farmers continue to demand agricultural subsidies; retirees, Medicare; home owners, subsidized mortgages; and college students, loans. We insist upon a national security state to protect against terrorism, generous Social Security benefits at an early retirement age, federal highways, and a vast system of national parks. But we don't want a lot of *government*.

The Ronald Reagan Legacy Project, which is working to have a public facility named after the fortieth president in each of the country's 3,067 counties, embodies this contradiction. "Public facility" is loosely interpreted in the case of the Ronald Reagan bust outside a McDonald's in Tuscaloosa County, Alabama. Elsewhere, buildings named after him are emblems of the expansive government role he rejected. No monument looms more ironically than the Ronald Reagan Building and International Trade Center in Washington, DC, which became the most expensive structure the federal government ever built when it was finished at a cost of $768 million in 1998. Here stands the vast bureaucratic testament to a man who said that if all the federal workers went away no one would miss them.

Reagan had two enormous and related blind spots. One was about the possibility of government serving as a positive force in people's lives. The other was about private enterprise serving as a negative one. Like his hostility toward Washington, Reagan's faith in the free market went too far. Religious voluntarism and personal generosity weren't substitutes for the Great Society, however flawed some of its programs were. Deregulation and pro-business policies unleashed enormous entrepreneurial energies. But they also provided opportunities for the unscrupulous to take advantage. The financial crisis of 2008, driven by irresponsible risk taking and self-regulation, was an indirect consequence of Reaganism.

The country Reagan left behind was a different place than it was when he took office: more confident but more selfish, better at generating wealth but worse at distributing it widely. In a fundamental sense, it was less democratic. It's no use pretending that we could somehow have had the positive aspects of this transformation without the negative ones, the growth without the greed. Reagan took the self-seeking and hedonism of the 1970s and transmuted them into financial aspirations. His economically liberated America was a place where it was easier to become rich, and where people cared more about becoming rich. The social impact of his actions was anything but conservative, accelerating the move away from the traditional community he hearkened back to and fueling a new culture of media and celebrity. Given the choice, Reagan didn't want to live in that closed, small-town world, either. He wanted to preserve what was best about it as part of the national ideal.

Like his early hero Franklin Roosevelt, Reagan became president at a moment when the country's future looked bleak. He sought to revive morale through both a set of policies and a reassertion of the nation's values. He led the United States to victory in a global conflict, leaving it atop the world as a lone superpower and victor in the battle of ideas. Ronald Reagan believed that the United States was always and everywhere a force for good in the world. When it succeeds in serving as one, it looks to the best part of his legacy. When it falls short of that standard, it reminds us of the worst.

Notes

INTRODUCTION: SURROUNDED BY A WALL OF LIGHT

2   "It was a humbling feeling": Ronald Reagan diary entry for July 27, 1987, Reagan Library.

4   "I, every person I interviewed": Edmund Morris, interview with Lesley Stahl, *60 Minutes*, Oct. 10, 1999.

5   "There's a wall around him": Nancy Reagan, *My Turn* (New York: Random House, 1989), 106.

6   "They are not 'the masses'": Kiron K. Skinner, Annelise Anderson, and Martin Anderson, eds., *Reagan in His Own Hand* (New York: The Free Press, 2001), 18.

6   "optimistic imagination": Lou Cannon, *President Reagan: The Role of a Lifetime* (1991; repr., New York: PublicAffairs, 2000), 194.

6   "I hate them to this day": Ronald Reagan, *Where's the Rest of Me?* (1965; repr., New York: Dell, 1981), 25.

6   "surrounded by a wall of light": "Dutch Makes His First Scene," *Des Moines Sunday Register*, June 27, 1937.

1: FACT AND FANCY

9   "something of an outcast": Stephen Vaughn, *Ronald Reagan in Hollywood: Movies and Politics* (New York: Cambridge University Press, 1994), 57.

10   Carrie Nation was a Disciple: Garry Wills, *Reagan's America: Innocents at Home* (New York: Doubleday, 1987), 20–32.

10   "There were times when he didn't open the screen door": Lou Cannon, *Governor Reagan: His Rise to Power* (New York: PublicAffairs, 2003), 14.

10   Nancy Reagan attributed the lack of close friends: Nancy Reagan, *My Turn*, 106.

11   Jack drank away the money: Patti Davis, *The Way I See It* (G. P. Putnam's Sons, 1992), 12.

11   "two hundred yards wide and endlessly long": Reagan, *Where's the Rest of Me?*, 24.

12   "an abiding belief in the triumph of good over evil": Jerry Griswold, "Young Reagan's Reading," *New York Times Book Review*, Aug. 30, 1981.

12   "I got a fistful of his overcoat": Reagan, *Where's the Rest of Me?*, 12.

12   "used to love to make up plays": Anne Edwards, *Early Reagan: The Rise to Power* (New York: William Morrow, 1987), 63.

13   "Everyone had to look at me": "New Answer to Maidens' Prayers," *Motion Picture*, Dec. 1939, 85.

14   "Ours was no riotous burning in effigy": Reagan, *Where's the Rest of Me?*, 34.

14   "No memories of scholarship": Cannon, *Governor Reagan*, 32.

14   ending up as an athletic coach at a small school: "New Answer to Maidens' Prayers."

15   "bathed in the blood of youth": Edmund Morris, *Dutch* (New York: Random House, 1999), 100.

15   "It deals with the Ku Klux Klan": Reagan, *Where's the Rest of Me?*, 13.

16   She read his sunniness as a lack of ambition: Edwards, *Early Reagan*, 99.

16   "As our lives traveled into divergent paths": Reagan, *Where's the Rest of Me?*, 55.

16   "He had an inability to distinguish between fact and fancy": Morris, *Dutch*, 121.

2: SIGN BEFORE THEY CHANGE THEIR MINDS

17   "world famous collection of spines": Vaughn, *Ronald Reagan in Hollywood*, 24.

18   send-ups of President Roosevelt's Fireside Chats: Edwards, *Early Reagan*, 149.

18   "painting a word picture": Richard Reeves, *President Reagan: The Triumph of Imagination* (New York: Simon and Schuster, 2005), 207.

18   Reagan would gyrate in the recording booth: "Daughters Recall Tales of Mom Dating Reagan," *Waterloo–Cedar Falls Courier*, Feb. 3, 2011.

20   more fan mail than any star: Vaughn, *Ronald Reagan in Hollywood*, 79.

21   "averageness" was his key asset: Cannon, *Governor Reagan*, 67.

21   "Mr. Norm is my alias": "How to Make Yourself Important," *Photoplay*, August 1942, 44.

21   likely a fabrication of Rockne's: Murray Sperber, *Shake Down the Thunder: The Creation of Notre Dame Football* (1993; repr., Bloomington: Indiana University Press, 2002), 112.

22 "And right from the start": "How to Make Yourself Important."

23 "the principles America lives by": Vaughn, *Ronald Reagan in Hollywood*, 222.

23 "With parts I've had": "Postwar Reagan," *Picturegoer*, July 19, 1947. Cited in Vaughn, *Ronald Reagan in Hollywood*, 231.

23 "they'd cast me as a lawyer from the east": *Los Angeles Daily News*, July 24, 1950. Cited in Vaughn, *Ronald Reagan in Hollywood*, 231.

3: THE ONLY VOICE FOR REAL LIBERALS

25 Neil later boasted about spying: Wills, *Reagan's America*, 291–92.

25 his FBI file later revealed: "Reagan Acted as Informant for FBI," *San Jose Mercury News*, Aug. 25, 1985.

26 he reported back to SAG: Vaughn, *Ronald Reagan in Hollywood*, 154.

26 "the only voice for real liberals": Ibid., 168.

28 "here in Hollywood we licked the Communists": Reagan to Orvil Dryfoos, Oct. 16, 1962, *New York Times* company records, Autograph file, Manuscripts and Archives Division, New York Public Library.

28 "newspaper in hand, expounding": Father Robert Perrella, *They Call Me the Showbiz Priest* (New York: Trident Press, 1973), cited in Cannon, *Governor Reagan*, 74.

29 "Ronnie is not a sophisticated fellow": Cannon, *Governor Reagan*, 73.

29 waking up with starlets: Kitty Kelley, *Nancy Reagan: The Unauthorized Biography* (New York: Pocket Books, 1992), 78.

29 "It took him a long time": Cannon, *Governor Reagan*, 79.

29 "a mild state of rapture": Davis, *The Way I See It*, 43.

30 "You can get just so far to Ronnie, and then something happens": Cannon, *President Reagan*, 192.

30 "I, in my own mind": "America the Beautiful," June 1952, collected in Davis W. Houck and Amos Kiewe, eds., *Actor, Ideologue, Politician: The Public Speeches of Ronald Reagan* (Westport, CT: Greenwood Press, 1993), 6.

31 One possible source: Vaughn, *Ronald Reagan in Hollywood*, 116.

32 "Never mind, son, we'll ride it down together": "America the Beautiful," 8.

4: LIVING BETTER ELECTRICALLY

34 "postgraduate course in political science": Ronald Reagan, *An American Life* (New York: Simon and Schuster, 1990), 129.

35 "when you live better electrically": Horace Newcomb, ed., *Encyclopedia of Television* (New York: Routledge, 2013), 970.

36 "telling the workers what they are entitled to": Joan Cook, "Lemuel

Ricketts Boulware, 95; Headed Labor Relations for G.E.," *New York Times*, Nov. 8, 1990.

36 enlisting them as "mass communicators": Thomas W. Evans, *The Education of Ronald Reagan* (New York: Columbia University Press, 2006), 4.

37 "didn't want to be at a loss to discuss it": Interview with Earl B. Dunckel, 1982, Regional Oral History Office, Bancroft Library, University of California at Berkeley, 30.

37 "government interference and snafus": Reagan, *An American Life*, 129.

37 "came to the realization that he was no longer a Democrat": Dunckel interview, 22.

37 "something inherent in government": Ronald Reagan, Commencement Address at Eureka College, June 7, 1957.

38 "the stultifying hand of government regulation and interference": "Business, Ballots, and Bureaus," May 1959, collected in Houck and Kiewe, eds., *Actor, Ideologue, Politician*, 19.

38 "I had completed the process of self-conversion": Reagan, *An American Life*, 134.

39 "If someone is setting fire to the house": Ronald Reagan, television address, Nov. 4, 1962. Collected in Houck and Kiewe, eds., *Actor, Ideologue, Politician*, 28.

39 Cordiner said that would make his life easier: Reagan, *Where's the Rest of Me?*, 306.

40 making model changes "to sustain public interest": J. Stanford Smith to Taft Schreiber, March 30, 1962, "General Electric" folder, Reagan Library.

40 "In token of our appreciation": J. Stanford Smith to Ronald Reagan, April 25, 1962, "General Electric" folder, Reagan Library.

41 the employees "you gentlemen were engaged with recently": Dan Moldea, *Dark Victory: Ronald Reagan, MCA, and the Mob* (New York: Viking, 1986), 193.

5: I'VE NEVER PLAYED A GOVERNOR

43 " 'My name is Ronald Reagan,' Dad said": Michael Reagan with Joe Hyams, *On the Outside Looking In* (New York: Zebra Books, 1988), 96.

43 "Why do you make these things up about your mother?" and "I couldn't find my father": Davis, *The Way I See It*, 150, 21.

43 "I could share an hour of warm camaraderie with Dad": Ron Reagan, *My Father at 100* (New York: Viking, 2011), 8–9.

44 encouraged them to quote from it extensively: Morris, *Dutch*, 335–36.

45 "the most successful political debut since William Jennings Bryan":

Stephen Hess and David S. Broder, *The Republican Establishment: The Present and Future of the G.O.P.* (New York: Harper and Row, 1967), 253.

45   "the sacrifice of running for governor": Lou Cannon, *Ronnie and Jesse: A Political Odyssey* (Garden City, NY: Doubleday, 1969), 74.

46   without challenging popular benefits: Cannon, *Governor Reagan*, 157.

47   "You never shoot your own horse": Reeves, *President Reagan*, 117.

48   "Ronald Reagan receives the representative of 'Pravda' ": Desk files, Reagan Library.

48   "I'll sell my bonds": Cannon, *President Reagan*, 113.

49   doubling state spending on higher education: Cannon, *Governor Reagan*, 296.

49   "Anytime I can get 70 percent of what I'm asking for": Interview with Peter D. Hannaford in Kenneth W. Thompson, ed., *Leadership in the Reagan Presidency, Part II: Eleven Intimate Perspectives* (Lanham, MD: University Press of America, 1993), 155.

50   State revenues climbed: California Department of Finance, Historical Documents, available at www.dof.ca.gov.

6: CALL IT MYSTICISM

52   "You can call it mysticism if you want to": Ronald Reagan, speech to Conservative Political Action Conference, Washington, DC, Jan. 25, 1974.

53   "a banner of no pale pastels": Ronald Reagan, speech to Second Conservative Political Action Conference, Washington, DC, Feb. 15, 1975.

54   "shoddy treatment" of the vice president: Craig Shirley, *Reagan's Revolution: The Untold Story of the Campaign That Started It All* (Nashville, TN: Thomas Nelson, 2005), 42.

54   "become more intrusive": Cannon, *Governor Reagan*, 410.

54   "a citizen representing my fellow citizens": Ronald Reagan, announcement of presidential candidacy, National Press Club, Washington, DC, Nov. 20, 1975.

54   was actually white: Josh Levin, "The Welfare Queen," *Slate*, Dec. 19, 2013.

56   he had privately rehearsed: Ron Reagan, *My Father at 100*, 176.

56   "Will they look back with appreciation": Ronald Reagan, remarks at Republican National Convention, Kansas City, MO, Aug. 19, 1976.

7: I PAID FOR THAT MICROPHONE

57   "You've written this so it can be read": George Shultz, foreword to Skinner et al., eds., *Reagan in His Own Hand*, x.

58   "good natured, generous spirit": Ronald Reagan, "Letters to the

Editor," June 1975, in Skinner et al., eds., *Reagan in His Own Hand*, 15.

58 "the road our English cousins have already taken": "Shaping the World for 100 Years to Come," Sept. 1, 1976, in Skinner et al., eds., *Reagan in His Own Hand*, 10.

58 "if government would someday quietly close the doors": "Convention #1," Sept. 1, 1976, in Skinner et al., eds., *Reagan in His Own Hand*, 236.

58 "Apparently the Russians have a laser beam": Ronald Reagan, "Russians," May 25, 1977, in Skinner et al., eds., *Reagan in His Own Hand*, 34.

58 "their system will collapse": Ronald Reagan, "The Russian Wheat Deal," Oct. 1975, in Skinner et al., eds., *Reagan in His Own Hand*, 31.

59 "Written around 1962": Ronald Reagan, "Are Liberals Really Liberal?" desk archives, Box 1, Reagan Library. Skinner et al. speculate that it was written in 1963.

59 "Maybe we should drop a few million typical mail order catalogs": Ronald Reagan, "Soviet Workers," May 25, 1977, in Skinner et al., eds., *Reagan in His Own Hand*, 147.

60 the movement's most influential article: Jeane J. Kirkpatrick, "Dictatorships and Double Standards," *Commentary*, Nov. 1979.

60 "to press the button or do nothing": Martin Anderson, *Revolution* (San Diego, CA: Harcourt Brace Jovanovich, 1988), 83.

60 a "protective missile system": Ibid., 85.

61 peace treaties never lead to peace: Laurence Beilenson, *The Treaty Trap* (Washington, DC: Public Affairs Press, 1969).

61 "a small boy who has been dropped off at the wrong birthday party": William Loeb, quoted in Cannon, *Governor Reagan*, 462.

62 "one of the few political leaders I have met": Quoted in Helen Thomas, *Thanks for the Memories, Mr. President: Wit and Wisdom from the Front Row at the White House* (New York: Scribner, 2003), 128.

8: THE PRESENT CRISIS

67 "Who's Jack Warner?": Reeves, *President Reagan*, 2.

68 The parties cost $19.4 million: Whitney Gleaves, "Cost of Inaugurations," Jan. 21, 2005, Hauenstein Center for Presidential Studies.

70 "I'm trying to undo the 'Great Society'": Douglas Brinkley, ed., *The Reagan Diaries* (New York: Harper, 2007), 65.

71 "the greatest attempt of savings": Cannon, *President Reagan*, 203.

72 "something just short of a Bush-Baker *coup d'état*": James A. Baker III with Steve Fiffer, *"Work Hard, Study . . . and Keep Out of Politics!": Adventures and Lessons from an Unexpected Life* (New York: G. P. Putnam's Sons, 2006), 146.

73   pushed 400,000 people off the welfare rolls: Gareth Davies, "The Welfare State," in W. Elliot Brownlee and Hugh Davis Graham, eds., *The Reagan Presidency: Pragmatic Conservatism and Its Legacies* (Lawrence: University Press of Kansas, 2003), 211.

75   "trust my judgment on this one": Reeves, *President Reagan*, 75.

75   "trickle-down economics": William Greider, "The Education of David Stockman," *The Atlantic Monthly*, Dec. 1981.

75   "If true, David is a turncoat": Brinkley, ed., *Reagan Diaries*, 48.

75   "We who were going to balance the budget": Ibid., 53.

77   he got only a quarter of the cuts: Davies, "Welfare State," 218.

77   "not a budget issue": Morris, *Dutch*, 450.

78   the deficit would reach $208 billion: Office of Management and Budget, Historical Tables, www.whitehouse.gov/omb/budget /Historicals, accessed May 30, 2015.

9: I THINK I MADE A FRIEND

80   "staff-dependent": Reeves, *President Reagan*, 13.

81   "so intellectually disreputable": David Stockman, *The Triumph of Politics: Why the Reagan Revolution Failed* (New York: Harper and Row, 1986), 291.

84   "Young Mr. Andrews without hesitation leaped": Brinkley, ed., *Reagan Diaries*, 121.

84   "She was referring to abortion": Ibid., 218.

85   "I literally told him my life story": Ibid., 549.

86   "You mean our position should be, 'no tickee, no laundry'?": James Graham Wilson, *The Triumph of Improvisation: Gorbachev's Adaptability, Reagan's Engagement, and the End of the Cold War* (Ithaca, NY: Cornell University Press, 2014), 61.

10: THE ASH HEAP OF HISTORY

89   "Ten Commandments of Nikolai Lenin": Michael Dobbs, *Down with Big Brother: The Fall of the Soviet Union* (New York: Alfred A. Knopf, 1997), 143.

89   signed some of his early writings: Bertram D. Wolfe, *Three Who Made a Revolution* (New York: Dial, 1948), 153n.

89   "these false quotations that he is using": "Reagan Criticized for Human Rights Statements," Associated Press, May 31, 1988.

90   Reagan misunderstood the phrase: Raymond L. Garthoff, *The Great Transition: American-Soviet Relations and the End of the Cold War* (Washington, DC: Brookings Institution Press, 1994), 41.

91   "they've already got their people on a starvation diet": Ibid., 11.

91   "What I want is to bring them to their knees": John A. Farrell, *Tip*

O'Neill and the Democratic Century (Boston: Little, Brown, 2001), 607.

92 "not in some vague, long-range historical sense": Robert Gates, *From the Shadows: The Ultimate Insider's Story of Five Presidents and How They Won the Cold War* (1996; repr., New York: Simon and Schuster, 2007), 194.

92 "because it is contrary to human nature": Reagan, "Are Liberals Really Liberal?"

93 "Here is the 1st major break in the Red dike": Brinkley, ed., *Reagan Diaries*, 30.

93 "We can't let this revolution against Communism fail": Ibid., 58.

93 forgoing those that would hurt American companies: Wilson, *Triumph of Improvisation*, 30.

94 much of this language was Reagan's: Robert C. Rowland and John M. Jones, *Reagan at Westminster: Foreshadowing the End of the Cold War* (College Station, TX: Texas A&M University Press, 2010), chap. 2.

94 Reagan crossed out the words "now and forever": David Gergen, *Eyewitness to Power* (New York: Simon and Schuster, 2001), 242–43.

95 nuclear-size explosion in the Siberian wilderness: Thomas C. Reed, *At the Abyss: An Insider's History of the Cold War* (New York: Presidio Press, 2004), 269.

95 one of his favorite fake Lenin quotes: Reagan, *An American Life*, 474.

97 fell asleep while the pope was talking: Reeves, *President Reagan*, 107.

11: THEY KEEP DYING ON ME

98 Reagan dismissed the overture: Garthoff, *Great Transition*, 46.

98 God had saved him for the purpose of preventing nuclear war: Reagan, *An American Life*, 269.

99 "I need to follow my own instincts": Reeves, *President Reagan*, 54.

99 an "icy reply": Reagan, *An American Life*, 273.

100 He hadn't understood: Don Oberdorfer, *The Turn: From the Cold War to a New Era* (New York: Poseidon Press, 1991), 100.

101 "a very dangerous fraud": Speech to the National Association of Evangelicals, Orlando, FL, Mar. 8, 1983.

102 "every weapon has resulted in a defense": Reeves, *President Reagan*, 142.

102 Reagan latched on: Oberdorfer, *The Turn*, 27.

102 "the greatest sting operation in history": Frances FitzGerald, *Way Out There in the Blue: Reagan, Star Wars, and the End of the Cold War* (New York: Simon and Schuster, 2001), 519.

103   "protect our people not avenge them": Brinkley, ed., *Reagan Diaries*, 130.

103   Yuri Andropov, took it as confirmation: Wilson, *Triumph of Improvisation*, 73.

104   on the basis of a personal recommendation from Richard Nixon: Cannon, *President Reagan*, 78.

104   "he regarded it as his turf": Reagan, *An American Life*, 270.

105   "an outbreak of world peace": FitzGerald, *Way Out There in the Blue*, 222.

105   "I think I'm hard-line": Brinkley, ed., *Reagan Diaries*, 142.

106   Reagan begged him to stay: Wilson, *Triumph of Improvisation*, 75.

107   comparing him to Hitler: Oberdorfer, *The Turn*, 65.

107   Reagan had tears in his eyes: Reagan, *An American Life*, 456.

108   "get a top Soviet leader in a room alone": Brinkley, ed., *Reagan Diaries*, 259.

109   dismissed his warmer tone as an election-year ploy: Oberdorfer, *The Turn*, 73.

109   "I have a gut feeling I'd like to talk to him": Brinkley, ed., *Reagan Diaries*, 220.

110   "I think this calls for a very well thought out reply": Reagan letter to Chernenko, Box 39, Folder 8401238, Executive Secretariat NSC Head of State Files, 1981–89, Reagan Library.

12: MORNING AGAIN IN AMERICA

111   Clark thought he was slipping mentally: Reeves, *President Reagan*, 194.

113   "My heart sank as he floundered": "Ronald Reagan Had Alzheimer's While President, Says Son," *The Guardian*, Jan. 17, 2011.

115   Pat Schroeder of Colorado astutely observed: Pat Schroeder, "Nothing Stuck to 'Teflon' President," *USA Today*, June 6, 2004.

115   "sacramental vision": Hugh Heclo, "Ronald Reagan and the American Public Philosophy," in Brownlee and Graham, eds., *Reagan Presidency*, 17–37.

13: WHY WAIT UNTIL THE YEAR 2000?

119   "if we got rid of them entirely": "Election '84: An Interview with the President," *Time*, Nov. 19, 1984.

120   Soviet losses would be limited to a much smaller percentage: Reagan, *An American Life*, 550.

120   "as if they were talking about baseball scores": Ibid.

120   "we should both tone down public rhetoric": Head of State Files, Secretary Gorbachev, Box 39, Folder 8590272.

121 "George is carrying out my policy": Brinkley, ed., *Reagan Diaries*, 277.

121 led her all the way to Reagan: Suzanne Massie, *Trust but Verify: Reagan, Russia, and Me* (Rockland, ME: Hearttree Press, 2013).

121 at one point asking Paul Nitze: Oberdorfer, *The Turn*, 143.

122 "going through a spiritual revival": Brinkley, ed., *Reagan Diaries*, 412.

122 "the more charming the adversary": Wilson, *Triumph of Improvisation*, 89.

123 "some future madman": Head of State Files, Box 39, Folder 8590336.

124 "a Soviet leader I could talk to": Reagan, *An American Life*, 640–41.

125 "the most important channel": Head of State Files, Box 40, Folder 8591293.

125 "Why wait until the year 2000?": Oberdorfer, *The Turn*, 157.

125 "the president of the United States doesn't agree with you": George P. Shultz, *Turmoil and Triumph: My Years as Secretary of State* (New York: Charles Scribner's Sons, 1993), 699–705.

125 "keeping the negotiations machine running idle": Wilson, *Triumph of Improvisation*, 111.

127 "This does not mean a trade": Brinkley, ed., *Reagan Diaries*, 437.

127 why not the complete elimination of ballistic missiles?: Oberdorfer, *The Turn*, 197–98.

14: THE FACTS TELL ME

128 "targeted for a Communist takeover": Brinkley, ed., *Reagan Diaries*, 50.

130 "It just drove him crazy": George Shultz interview, 2005, Ronald Reagan Oral History, The Miller Center.

131 "I don't think I could forgive myself if we didn't try": H. W. Brands, *Reagan: The Life* (New York: Doubleday, 2015), 552.

131 He phoned Weir: *Public Papers of the Presidents of the United States: Administration of Ronald Reagan, 1985*, Office of the Federal Register, 1517.

131 "what are we doing to get my hostages?": Malcolm Byrne, *Iran-Contra: Reagan's Scandal and the Unchecked Abuse of Presidential Power* (Lawrence: University Press of Kansas, 2014), 40.

131 The two came bearing gifts: Ibid., 195.

132 the $3.8 million North was able to filch: Richard Sobel, "Contra Aid Fundamentals: Exploring the Intricacies and Issues," *Political Science Quarterly* 110, no. 2 (Summer 1995): 287–306.

133 "This may call for resignations": Reagan, *An American Life*, 530.

136 comparing Reagan's use of language: Visha Berisha et al., "Tracking Discourse Complexity Preceding Alzheimer's Disease Diagno-

sis: A Case Study Comparing the Press Conferences of Presidents Ronald Reagan and George Herbert Walker Bush," *Journal of Alzheimer's Disease* 45, no. 3 (2015).

136 "I can't remember the other two": Reeves, *President Reagan*, 403.

136 "people didn't believe me": Reagan, *An American Life*, 532.

139 dropped his camera: James Mann, *The Rebellion of Ronald Reagan* (New York: Viking, 2009), 193.

15: TEAR DOWN THIS WALL

140 a primitive, and a caveman: Brands, *Reagan*, 610.

141 an impenetrable nuclear shield was technologically unrealistic: Jack F. Matlock Jr., *Reagan and Gorbachev: How the Cold War Ended* (New York: Random House, 2004), 248.

141 "transparency of intent": Ibid., 320.

142 Reagan sent a personal letter: Head of State Files, Box 41, Folder 8790364.

143 "Howard, I think I'm the only person": Oberdorfer, *The Turn*, 244.

Milestones

1911 Ronald Wilson Reagan is born on February 6 in Tampico, Illinois.

1932 Graduates from Eureka College; begins work as a sports announcer for WOC radio in Davenport, Iowa.

1937 Signs contract with Warner Bros.; makes his first films.

1940 Marries fellow Warner contract player Jane Wyman; plays George Gipp in *Knute Rockne—All American*.

1941 Daughter Maureen is born.

1942 Delivers his most acclaimed performance in *Kings Row*; is drafted into Army Air Forces and assigned to the First Motion Picture Unit.

1945 Adopts son Michael.

1947 Is elected president of Screen Actors Guild; testifies before House Un-American Activities Committee.

1949 Reagan and Wyman divorce.

1952 Marries Nancy Davis; daughter Patti is born.

1954 Begins hosting *General Electric Theater* and working as traveling spokesman for GE.

1958 Son Ron Jr. is born.

1962 Officially changes his party registration from Democratic to Republican.

1964 Gives television address "A Time for Choosing" on behalf of Barry Goldwater.

1965 Publishes first autobiography, *Where's the Rest of Me?*

1966   Defeats incumbent California governor Edmund G. "Pat" Brown in a landslide.

1968   Briefly runs for president at Republican convention in Miami.

1969   Orders National Guard to break up protests at the University of California at Berkeley's People's Park.

1970   Is reelected governor of California.

1975   Writes syndicated newspaper column and radio commentaries; announces presidential candidacy.

1976   Loses Republican presidential nomination to Gerald Ford.

1979   Announces presidential candidacy.

1980   Wins Republican presidential nomination; chooses George Herbert Walker Bush as his running mate; defeats Jimmy Carter in landslide election.

1981   Is sworn in as the fortieth president on January 20.

Is shot by John Hinckley Jr. leaving a Washington hotel; recovers after surgery.

Passes economic program including 25 percent cut in tax rates, increases in defense spending, and cuts in social programs.

Fires striking air traffic controllers.

Appoints Sandra Day O'Connor as the first female justice on the U.S. Supreme Court.

1982   Replaces Alexander Haig with George P. Shultz as secretary of state.

Economy sinks into deep recession; agrees to first tax increase.

1983   Describes the USSR as an "evil empire" in a speech to the National Association of Evangelicals.

Unveils proposal for a Strategic Defense Initiative in a televised speech.

Two hundred forty-one U.S. Marines serving in peacekeeping force in Beirut die in truck bombing.

Authorizes invasion of Grenada.

1984   Urges help for Contra rebels in Nicaragua; Congress bans military aid.

Defeats Walter Mondale in landslide for reelection as president.

1985   Second term begins on January 20.

Holds first summit with Soviet leader Mikhail Gorbachev, in Geneva; proposes 50 percent cut in nuclear arms.

1986   Undergoes surgery for colon polyps.

The U.S. space shuttle *Challenger* explodes on takeoff.

Orders air strikes against Libya in retaliation for the bombing of a West Berlin disco.

Nominates Antonin Scalia to Supreme Court and elevates William H. Rehnquist to chief justice.

Meets Gorbachev for second time at summit in Reykjavik, Iceland, which ends without agreement.

Admits sending weapons to Iran but denies arms-for-hostages trade; Iran-Contra scandal widens.

Nancy Reagan is diagnosed with breast cancer and undergoes surgery.

Signs immigration and tax reform legislation.

1987   Tower Commission report on Iran-Contra blames Reagan for poor management.

In a speech at Berlin's Brandenburg Gate, demands that Gorbachev "tear down this wall."

Supreme Court nomination of Robert Bork fails, as does nomination of Douglas Ginsburg; nominates Anthony Kennedy.

Signs Intermediate-Range Nuclear Forces treaty with Gorbachev in Washington.

1988   Oliver North, John Poindexter, and two others are indicted by a federal grand jury.

Visits Soviet Union for final summit with Gorbachev.

George H. W. Bush defeats Massachusetts governor Michael Dukakis in presidential election.

1989   George H. W. Bush is inaugurated as forty-first president; Reagan returns to California.

Berlin Wall comes down.

1990   Publishes second autobiography, *An American Life*.

1991   Soviet Union is formally dissolved.

1994   Discloses in a letter to the public that he has Alzheimer's disease.

2004   Dies in California on June 5 at the age of ninety-three.

Selected Bibliography

Adelman, Ken. *Reagan at Reykjavik: Forty-Eight Hours That Ended the Cold War.* New York: Broadside Books, 2014.

Anderson, Martin. *Revolution.* San Diego: Harcourt Brace Jovanovich, 1988.

Baker, James A., III, with Steve Fiffer, *"Work Hard, Study . . . and Keep Out of Politics!": Adventures and Lessons from an Unexpected Life.* New York: G. P. Putnam's Sons, 2006.

Barrett, Laurence I. *Gambling with History: Reagan in the White House.* New York: Doubleday, 1983.

Boyarsky, Bill. *The Rise of Ronald Reagan.* New York: Random House, 1968.

Brands, H. W. *Reagan: The Life.* New York: Doubleday, 2015.

Brinkley, Douglas. *Gerald R. Ford.* New York: Times Books, 2007.

———, ed. *The Reagan Diaries.* New York: Harper, 2007.

———, ed. *Ronald Reagan: The Notes.* New York: Harper, 2011.

Brownlee, W. Elliot, and Hugh Davis Graham, eds. *The Reagan Presidency: Pragmatic Conservatism and Its Legacies.* Lawrence: University Press of Kansas, 2003.

Bruck, Connie, *When Hollywood Had a King: The Reign of Lew Wasserman, Who Leveraged Talent into Power and Influence.* New York: Random House, 2003.

Buckley, William F., Jr. *The Reagan I Knew.* New York: Basic Books, 2008.

Byrne, Malcolm. *Iran-Contra: Reagan's Scandal and the Unchecked Abuse of Presidential Power.* Lawrence: University Press of Kansas, 2014.

Cannon, Lou. *Governor Reagan: His Rise to Power.* New York: PublicAffairs, 2003.

———. *President Reagan: The Role of a Lifetime.* 1991; repr., New York: PublicAffairs, 2000.

———. *Reagan.* New York: G. P. Putnam's Sons, 1982.

———. *Ronnie and Jesse: A Political Odyssey.* Garden City, NY: Doubleday, 1969.

Colacello, Bob. *Ronnie and Nancy: Their Path to the White House, 1911–1980.* New York: Warner Books, 2004.

Dallek, Matthew W. *The Right Moment: Ronald Reagan's First Victory and the Decisive Turning Point in American Politics.* New York: The Free Press, 2000.

Darman, Jonathan. *Landslide: LBJ and Ronald Reagan at the Dawn of a New America.* New York: Random House, 2014.

Davis, Patti. *The Way I See It.* New York: G. P. Putnam's Sons, 1992.

Deaver, Michael K. *A Different Drummer: My Thirty Years with Ronald Reagan.* New York: HarperCollins, 2001.

Deaver, Michael K., with Mickey Herskowitz. *Behind the Scenes.* New York: William Morrow, 1987.

Diggins, John Patrick. *Ronald Reagan: Fate, Freedom, and the Making of History.* New York: W. W. Norton, 2007.

Dobbs, Michael. *Down with Big Brother: The Fall of the Soviet Empire.* New York: Alfred A. Knopf, 1997.

Draper, Theodore. *A Very Thin Line: The Iran-Contra Affairs.* New York: Hill and Wang, 1991.

Edwards, Anne. *Early Reagan: The Rise to Power.* New York: William Morrow, 1987.

———. *The Reagans: Portrait of a Marriage.* New York: St. Martin's Press, 2003.

Evans, Thomas W. *The Education of Ronald Reagan.* New York: Columbia University Press, 2006.

Farrell, John A. *Tip O'Neill and the Democratic Century.* Boston: Little, Brown, 2001.

FitzGerald, Frances. *Way Out There in the Blue: Reagan, Star Wars, and the End of the Cold War.* New York: Simon and Schuster, 2001.

Garthoff, Raymond L. *The Great Transition: American-Soviet Relations and the End of the Cold War.* Washington, DC: Brookings Institution Press, 1994.

Gates, Robert M. *From the Shadows: The Ultimate Insider's Story of Five Presidents and How They Won the Cold War.* 1996; repr., New York: Simon and Schuster, 2007.

Gergen, David. *Eyewitness to Power.* New York: Simon and Schuster, 2001.

Grachev, Andrei. *Gorbachev's Gamble: Soviet Foreign Policy and the End of the Cold War.* Cambridge, UK: Polity Press, 2008.

Greider, William. *The Education of David Stockman and Other Americans.* New York: E. P. Dutton, 1982.

Haig, Alexander M., Jr. *Caveat: Realism, Reagan, and Foreign Policy.* New York: Charles Scribner's Sons, 1984.

Holden, Ken. *The Making of the Great Communicator: Ronald Reagan's Transformation from Actor to Governor.* Guilford, CT: Lyons Press, 2013.

Houck, Davis W., and Amos Kiewe, eds. *Actor, Ideologue, Politician: The Public Speeches of Ronald Reagan.* Westport, CT: Greenwood Press, 1993.

Kengor, Paul. *God and Ronald Reagan: A Spiritual Life.* New York: Regan Books, 2004.

Kengor, Paul, and Patricia Clark Doerner. *The Judge: William P. Clark, Reagan's Top Hand.* San Francisco, CA: Ignatius Press, 2007.

Kuhn, Jim. *Ronald Reagan in Private: A Memoir of My Years in the White House.* New York: Sentinel, 2004.

Mann, James. *The Rebellion of Ronald Reagan: A History of the End of the Cold War.* New York: Viking, 2009.

Massie, Suzanne. *Trust but Verify: Reagan, Russia, and Me.* Rockland, ME: Hearttree Press, 2013.

Matlock, Jack F., Jr. *Reagan and Gorbachev: How the Cold War Ended.* New York: Random House, 2004.

McDougal, Dennis. *The Last Mogul: Lew Wasserman, MCA, and the Hidden History of Hollywood.* New York: Crown, 1998.

McFarlane, Robert C., with Zofia Smardz. *Special Trust.* New York: Cadell and Davies, 1994.

Meese, Edwin, III. *With Reagan: The Inside Story.* Washington, DC: Regnery Gateway, 1992.

Moldea, Dan E. *Dark Victory: Ronald Reagan, MCA, and the Mob.* New York: Viking, 1986.

Morella, Joe, and Edward Z. Epstein. *Jane Wyman: A Biography.* New York: Delacorte Press, 1985.

Morris, Edmund. *Dutch: A Memoir of Ronald Reagan.* New York: Random House, 1999.

Moynihan, Daniel Patrick. *Came the Revolution: Argument in the Reagan Era.* San Diego: Harcourt Brace Jovanovich, 1988.

Nofziger, Lyn. *Nofziger.* Washington, DC: Regnery Gateway, 1992.

Noonan, Peggy. *What I Saw at the Revolution: A Political Life in the Reagan Era.* Originally published 1990. New York: Random House, 2003.

———. *When Character Was King: A Story of Ronald Reagan.* New York: Viking, 2001.

Oberdorfer, Don. *The Turn: From the Cold War to a New Era.* New York: Poseidon Press, 1991.

Perlstein, Rick. *Before the Storm: Barry Goldwater and the Unmaking of the American Consensus.* New York: Hill and Wang, 2001.

———. *The Invisible Bridge: The Fall of Nixon and the Rise of Reagan.* New York: Simon and Schuster, 2014.

Reagan, Maureen. *First Father, First Daughter: A Memoir.* Boston: Little, Brown, 1989.

Reagan, Michael, with Joe Hyams. *On the Outside Looking In.* New York: Zebra Books, 1988.

Reagan, Nancy, with William Novak. *My Turn: The Memoirs of Nancy Reagan.* New York: Random House, 1989.

Reagan, Ron. *My Father at 100: A Memoir.* New York: Viking, 2011.

Reagan, Ronald. *An American Life.* New York: Simon and Schuster, 1990.

Reagan, Ronald, and Richard G. Hubler. *Where's the Rest of Me?* New York: E. P. Dutton, 1965.

Reed, Thomas C. *At the Abyss: An Insider's History of the Cold War.* New York: Presidio Press, 2004.

Reeves, Richard. *President Reagan: The Triumph of Imagination.* New York: Simon and Schuster, 2005.

Regan, Donald T. *For the Record: From Wall Street to Washington.* New York: Harcourt Brace Jovanovich, 1988.

Rowland, Robert C., and John M. Jones. *Reagan at Westminster: Foreshadowing the End of the Cold War.* College Station, TX: Texas A&M University Press, 2010.

Schweizer, Peter. *Reagan's War: The Epic Story of His Forty-Year Struggle and Final Triumph over Communism.* New York: Anchor Books, 2003.

Shirley, Craig. *Reagan's Revolution: The Untold Story of the Campaign That Started It All.* Nashville, TN: Thomas Nelson, 2005.

Shultz, George P. *Turmoil and Triumph: My Years as Secretary of State.* New York: Charles Scribner's Sons, 1993.

Skinner, Kiron K., Annelise Anderson, and Martin Anderson, eds. *Reagan: A Life in Letters.* New York: The Free Press, 2003.

———, eds. *Reagan in His Own Hand*. New York: The Free Press, 2001.

———, eds. *Reagan's Path to Victory*. New York: The Free Press, 2004.

Stockman, David. *The Triumph of Politics: Why the Reagan Revolution Failed*. New York: Harper and Row, 1986.

Strober, Deborah Hart, and Gerald S. Strober. *Reagan: The Man and His Presidency*. Boston: Houghton Mifflin, 1998.

Thomas, Helen. *Thanks for the Memories, Mr. President*. New York: Scribner, 2002.

Thompson, Kenneth W., ed. *Leadership in the Reagan Presidency: Seven Intimate Perspectives*. Lanham, MD: Madison Books, 1992.

———, ed. *Leadership in the Reagan Presidency, Part II: Eleven Intimate Perspectives*. Lanham, MD: University Press of America, 1993.

Traub, James. *Too Good to Be True: The Outlandish Story of Wedtech*. New York: Doubleday, 1990.

Troy, Gil. *Morning in America: How Ronald Reagan Invented the 1980s*. Princeton, NJ: Princeton University Press, 2003.

———. *The Reagan Revolution: A Very Short Introduction*. New York: Oxford University Press, 2009.

Vaughn, Stephen. *Ronald Reagan in Hollywood: Movies and Politics*. New York: Cambridge University Press, 1994.

Wallison, Peter J. *Ronald Reagan: The Power of Conviction and the Success of His Presidency*. Boulder, CO: Westview Press, 2004.

Weinberger, Caspar. *Fighting for Peace: Seven Critical Years at the Pentagon*. New York: Warner Books, 1991.

Wilentz, Sean. *The Age of Reagan: A History 1974–2008*. New York: Harper, 2008.

Wills, Garry. *Reagan's America: Innocents at Home*. New York: Doubleday, 1987.

Wilson, James Graham. *The Triumph of Improvisation: Gorbachev's Adaptability, Reagan's Engagement, and the End of the Cold War*. Ithaca, NY: Cornell University Press, 2014.

Zelizer, Julian E. *Jimmy Carter*. New York: Times Books, 2010.

Acknowledgments

Sean Wilentz and Paul Golob offered me this irresistible project and guided me through it. I'm grateful for their encouragement, their historical learning, and their editorial skill.

I rely on the advice and advocacy of my agent, Andrew Wylie. My friends Malcolm Gladwell, Michael Lewis, and David Plotz all read a draft of my manuscript and offered valuable suggestions. In the midst of his own exploration of the Reagan era on *The Americans*, my brother Joe Weisberg made time to go through it with a fine-tooth comb.

The staff at the Reagan Library in Simi Valley was welcoming and helpful during my visit there. Thanks go to John Heubusch and Jennifer Mandel, and to Joanne Drake of the Ronald Reagan Foundation for permission to quote from Reagan's prepresidential papers. I also wish to thank Gary Sheffer at General Electric and Tal Nadan at the Manuscripts and Archives Division of the New York Public Library.

My wonderful colleagues at *Slate*, Julia Turner, Dan Check, Brendan Monaghan, Matt Turck, and Ava Lubell, made allowances and covered for me during absences.

Final words of gratitude go to my wife, Deborah Needleman, and to my children, Lily and Nate. I couldn't have written this book without their love and indulgence.

Index

ABOUT THE AUTHOR

———

JACOB WEISBERG is chairman of the Slate Group and the former editor of *Slate* magazine. He is the author of *The Bush Tragedy* and the creator of the Bushisms series, among other books. Weisberg previously worked for *The New Republic* and was a contributing writer for *The New York Times Magazine,* a contributing editor to *Vanity Fair,* and a columnist for the *Financial Times.* He lives in New York City.